Unspoken

The Silent Crisis of Men's Mental Health in a Godless Age

By

D. M. Gross

UNSPOKEN: THE SILENT CRISIS OF MEN'S MENTAL HEALTH IN A GODLESS AGE

First edition. July 21, 2025.

ISBN: 979-8230548553

Written by D. M. Gross.

Table of Contents

Disclaimer

I am not a doctor, therapist, or licensed mental health professional. This book is not intended to diagnose, treat, or cure any medical or psychological condition. It is a work of research, observation, and personal reflection based on publicly available data, expert sources, and real human stories. While I've done my best to ensure accuracy and honesty, this book should not be used as a substitute for professional help. If you or someone you know is struggling with mental health, please seek guidance from a qualified healthcare provider or mental health professional. You deserve real support.

INTRODUCTION

The Things We Don't Say

There's a silence that eats men alive, and the worst part is—we taught them to starve in it. Not with knives or fists or wars, though those come later. No, the real violence starts quietly. It starts when a little boy hears, "Don't cry." It deepens when pain becomes shame, when emotion gets filed under weakness, when the only acceptable feeling left is anger. It sharpens in adolescence, hardens in adulthood, and calcifies in middle age until the man barely knows he's bleeding—because he's never been taught how to recognize the wound. He just knows he's tired. Or numb. Or furious for reasons he can't explain. And eventually, some just vanish—first emotionally, then socially, sometimes fatally. This book is about that silence. About the men it consumes. And about why, in this era of performative awareness and hashtags, the crisis facing men's mental health is still being brushed aside, joked about, politicized, or ignored—especially among the non-religious, where institutional refuge is even harder to find. You don't need to believe in a higher power to hurt. You don't need a Bible to break. And the truth is, men are breaking everywhere. Quietly. Daily. Systemically.

Statistically, the data punches hard: men account for nearly 80% of all suicide deaths in the United States. That's not a typo. The CDC confirms that men die by suicide at a rate nearly four times that of women, and the number spikes in key demographics—middle-aged white men, military veterans, divorced men, LGBTQ+ men, and men in economic distress. Meanwhile, men are significantly less likely to seek therapy, less likely to have strong emotional support networks, and more likely to mask psychological pain with socially accepted behaviors like overworking, binge drinking, or simply becoming emotionally unavailable. But here's the kicker: it's not because men "don't want to talk." It's because for decades—centuries, really—society hasn't made it safe or culturally acceptable for them to do so without facing ridicule, suspicion, or rejection. Emotional suppression was never a biological destiny. It was a social survival tactic.

Let's name something uncomfortable: the conversation around mental health is often more inclusive in theory than in practice. There's been a tremendous cultural push—rightfully so—toward de-stigmatizing mental health struggles, especially in marginalized groups. But in the process, a strange paradox has emerged: while advocating for compassion and nuance in mental health, many still treat male suffering as punchline, pathology, or privilege. Men are told they're the problem. That their pain is rooted in patriarchy. That their complaints are fragile. That their struggles pale in comparison to systemic injustice. But trauma doesn't cancel out trauma. And vulnerability doesn't need a purity test. The truth is, men are hurting in ways that aren't always visible, socially palatable, or even easily verbalized—and dismissing that hurt only deepens the crisis. Yes, men are more likely to cause harm. But they're also more likely to self-destruct silently. Both realities can be true at once. We don't fix one by ignoring the other.

Now let's layer in another factor—arguably the elephant in the psych ward: what happens when men suffer without a faith framework? For centuries, religion gave men a language for pain, a community to fall into, and rituals to help make sense of suffering. That wasn't always healthy—some faith systems did more damage than good—but it offered a scaffold. Today, especially in the West, more men than ever are identifying as atheist, agnostic, or "nones." Pew Research shows that roughly 34% of men under 30 are religiously unaffiliated. But unlike women, who often form strong social bonds outside of religious life, men tend to lose that community net entirely. When faith falls away, there's no automatic replacement. No tribe. No elders. No emotional vocabulary. Just a void where meaning used to be. So what do they do? Some isolate. Some numb out. Some look for answers in online rabbit holes or hyper-masculine echo chambers that promise control, order, and validation—but at the cost of compassion, nuance, or actual healing.

This book is not a sermon. There's no altar call coming. It's not written from faith, nor is it written in hostility toward it. It's written in the raw space between belief and despair—a place many men live. It's for those who aren't looking for salvation, but are desperate for a lifeline. For men who believe in reason, evidence, and truth—but who still wake up wondering what the hell is wrong with them, why nothing feels worth doing anymore, and whether anyone would really notice if they disappeared. It's for the man who drinks too much and calls it stress. Who hasn't touched another human being in weeks. Who can't remember the last time he laughed—really laughed—and isn't sure he'd want to even if he could. It's for the men who don't pray, but still want to be whole. Who don't believe in sin, but know they've done damage. Who don't need heaven, but wish they knew how to get out of this particular hell.

We need to talk about why help feels so foreign to men. Why therapy sounds like a foreign language. Why admitting fear feels like surrender. Why showing pain feels like failure. And more importantly, why those instincts are not hardwired—they're inherited. Cultural. Learned. They're shaped by decades of messaging that says "real men" endure without complaint, succeed without help, and suffer without tears. We made strength a cage. We made stoicism a straightjacket. Then we called it masculinity. And when men break down, we blame them for not asking for help—without ever teaching them the words, the place, or the permission to ask.

What's worse, even when men do ask, the system often fails them. Mental healthcare in most countries, especially the U.S., is overpriced, understaffed, and largely modeled on frameworks that don't always resonate with the way men experience distress. Studies show men are more likely to respond to solution-focused therapy, but many clinicians are trained in talk-heavy, emotion-centered models that feel alienating or ineffective. Some men get labeled "resistant" or "non-compliant" when in reality, the therapy just doesn't meet them where they are. Others walk away after one bad session, convinced the whole thing's a scam or a soft trap. And let's not pretend this issue is confined to therapy rooms. The culture at large—media, workplace, politics, relationships—still treats male vulnerability as a liability. Cry in public as a man and see how many people rush to comfort you versus how many glance, freeze, and look away. Society doesn't know what to do with hurting men—except ignore them until they become a headline.

So here's what we're going to do differently. We're going to talk in plain language. We're going to use hard data and hard truth. We're going to leave religion at the door—not out of disrespect, but out of relevance. We're going to pull from psychology, neuroscience, sociology, and lived experience to show that men's mental health is not just a "man problem," it's a human crisis with consequences that ripple across families, workplaces, economies, and generations. We're going to show how shame becomes silence, how silence becomes sickness, and how sickness becomes collapse. And we're going to do it without fluff, without euphemism, and without the patronizing tone that so often infects the way people talk about men's issues. This isn't about whining. It's about waking up.

Each part of this book will break open a different layer of the crisis. We'll begin with the numbers—because data doesn't care about your opinion. Then we'll dig into where it all starts: the culture, the childhoods, the father wounds, the social disconnect. We'll explore the hidden symptoms—how depression in men rarely looks like sadness and often masquerades as rage, workaholism, addiction, or quiet resignation. Then we'll pivot to what actually helps. Therapy that works. Communities that don't require belief. Philosophies that give structure to suffering without demanding worship. Finally, we'll cast our eyes forward: how we raise better sons, support marginalized men, and unlearn a legacy of emotional illiteracy that's killing us slowly.

Make no mistake—this isn't just a men's book. It's for anyone who loves a man, raises a man, dates a man, works with men, or is one. Because while men may suffer in silence, their silence screams through broken homes, burned-out employees, violent outbursts, or complete withdrawals. It shows up in the dad who's physically present but emotionally absent. In the friend who vanishes slowly over months. In the husband who explodes over nothing. In the coworker who just... stops showing up. And yes, in the funeral announcements that don't say "suicide," but say "sudden" or "unexpected" or nothing at all.

The old myth says men don't talk. That's false. Men talk all the time. But they need the right conditions. The right language. The right space. And most of all, the right reason. This book hopes to help create that space. It's not about fixing men. It's about freeing them. From silence. From shame. From the belief that feeling is weakness. That emotion is a burden. That healing is for someone else. It's about giving men—especially those without a faith map—a road back to themselves.

So if you've felt it—the numbness, the isolation, the fire you can't explain, the ache you can't name—this is your mirror. If you've loved someone who's gone dark behind their eyes and you don't know why, this is your map. If you've laughed off pain, buried it under porn or performance or perfectionism, and wondered why it still eats at you at night, this is your reckoning. You don't have to believe in anything divine to believe that something better is possible. You don't need a holy book to rewrite your story. You just need truth, science, support—and the courage to say the thing most men were never taught how to say:

I'm not okay.

And I don't want to disappear.

CHAPTER 1

Dead Men Don't Cry: Suicide by the Numbers

There's a saying in the world of emergency responders—simple, clinical, and soaked in horror: "He didn't make a sound." It's how they describe a certain kind of death. Quick. Violent. Intentional. And, more often than not, male. The truth is, most men who take their lives don't give a speech, leave a trail of red flags, or cry for help in a language anyone else knows how to translate. They just vanish—abruptly, methodically, and with the kind of finality that makes headlines and leaves loved ones whispering "but he seemed fine." Except he wasn't. He hadn't been for a long time. He was just good at hiding it. Because that's what he was taught. This chapter is not a eulogy. It's an autopsy of the myth that men don't suffer, that men don't feel deeply, or that male suicide is some fringe issue tucked into the corners of tragedy. It's not. It's a global epidemic. And it's getting worse.

Let's strip this down to the data—cold and clinical, because we need to stop pretending this is a minor concern. In the United States, according to the CDC's most recent numbers, men account for nearly 80% of all completed suicides. To be exact, the suicide rate among men is roughly 3.9 times higher than that of women. That's not a rounding error. That's a cultural indictment. We're not talking about rare edge cases or mental instability confined to the margins—we're talking about sons, brothers, husbands, co-workers, neighbors. We're talking about veterans returning home from wars only to lose the battle in their own heads. We're talking about teenagers in rural towns with nowhere to turn. Middle-aged men whose jobs, marriages, or identities collapse and take their last threads of will with them. Elderly men isolated in nursing homes, forgotten. We're talking about professionals, blue-collar workers, single fathers, gay men rejected by families, trans men navigating identity and risk, disabled men invisible to the system. Suicide doesn't care how strong you look. It cares how silent you are.

But the silence is not organic—it's manufactured. Culturally programmed. From the youngest age, boys are flooded with messaging about what emotions are "acceptable," and more importantly, which ones aren't. Anger is fine. Rage is masculine. But sadness? Fear? Vulnerability? Those are to be crushed, hidden, or spun into sarcasm, stoicism, or shame. The result is that men are less likely to verbalize emotional pain, less likely to seek support, and far more likely to reach for permanent solutions to what could have been temporary suffering—if someone had taught them how to name it. This isn't conjecture. The National Institute of Mental Health notes that men are statistically far less likely than women to be diagnosed with depression—not because they don't experience it, but because male depression often manifests differently. It shows up as irritability, fatigue, withdrawal, aggression, or numbness—symptoms that get written off as personality flaws instead of cries for help. The DSM hasn't caught up. Neither has the average workplace, family, or friend group.

Now zoom out. Globally, the pattern repeats. In the UK, the Office for National Statistics reports that three out of four suicides are male. In Australia, men are three times more likely to die by suicide than women, despite similar rates of diagnosed mental illness. In Japan, where societal shame around failure and emotional disclosure runs deep, suicide has long been a cultural undercurrent—especially among older men. Even in countries with strong social support networks and universal healthcare, male suicide remains disproportionately high. Why? Because even the best systems don't matter if the men inside them have been taught that asking for help is weakness, or worse, failure.

We also have to talk about how men die. The methods are usually more violent, more final, more difficult to intervene. While women are more likely to attempt suicide, men are far more likely to succeed—largely because they use firearms, hanging, or jumping, rather than pills or cutting. It's not about intent. It's about conditioning. When a man decides to end his life, it's rarely a cry for help. It's often a calculated act performed with the same ruthless efficiency society once praised him for at work. Only this time, the task is self-erasure. And when it's over, we act shocked—because he didn't "seem the type."

But what is the type? We keep asking the wrong questions. We ask, "Why didn't he talk to someone?" instead of, "What made him believe he couldn't?" We ask, "What was wrong with him?" instead of, "What systems failed him?" We label him as mentally ill and move on, ignoring the fact that suicide is often less about pathology and more about pressure. Social, economic, existential. Pressure to perform. To provide. To stay strong. To be unshakable. To never let the mask slip. And when the mask starts to crack? Most men don't call a hotline. They call it quits.

And for some men, the risk spikes even higher. Let's talk veterans. According to the U.S. Department of Veterans Affairs, an average of 17–22 veterans die by suicide every single day. Think about that. That's a plane crash worth of deaths, daily, mostly unnoticed. These are men trained to endure unimaginable trauma, then tossed back into civilian life with little preparation and even less support. They're told to be proud, to be grateful, to be strong. But pride doesn't treat PTSD. And strength doesn't hug you at night when your mind is crawling with flashbacks. These are not just soldiers dying. They're husbands, fathers, friends—and they're not just casualties of war. They're casualties of silence. Of systems that celebrate their sacrifice but can't be bothered to catch them when they fall apart.

Then there are men in marginalized communities—LGBTQ+ men, Black men, Indigenous men, disabled men—who face double burdens. Not only are they fighting the internal weight of despair, but they're often up against racism, homophobia, transphobia, poverty, and systemic erasure. According to The Trevor Project's 2024 survey, 45% of LGBTQ+ youth seriously considered suicide in the past year, with transgender men and nonbinary individuals facing the highest risks. For them, it's not just about stigma. It's about rejection from families, harassment from peers, violence from strangers, and an internalized shame that festers where community should be. We don't just need better mental healthcare—we need a world that stops punishing men for not fitting its narrow definitions of "acceptable."

There's also the economic factor. Studies show a direct link between job loss, economic instability, and suicide risk in men. During the COVID-19 pandemic, suicide hotlines reported surges in male callers, especially in the 35–54 age bracket. When a man's identity is tied to work, and work disappears, so does his sense of worth. We've conditioned men to equate value with productivity. No job? No purpose. No income? No dignity. And because emotional literacy was never taught, and community ties have frayed, many men simply fold inward—cutting off from family, friends, even themselves, until what's left is a shell of someone no one can quite reach anymore.

This is not about blaming anyone. It's about confronting everyone. The culture. The conditioning. The conversations we never have. Because every time someone rolls their eyes at "men's issues," a man inches closer to thinking no one cares. Every time a guy says "I'm fine" and we don't push a little harder, another door shuts. Every time the media paints male vulnerability as pathetic or performative, another man decides silence is safer. The stigma isn't just external—it's internalized. Men police themselves more brutally than anyone else ever could.

Let's also be real about what men do instead of talk. They drink. They gamble. They disappear into porn, work, or risk. They self-medicate. They become adrenaline junkies or sex addicts or rage-filled cynics. Some weaponize their pain. Others dissolve in it. But most don't call it "depression." They call it life. Or stress. Or "just how it is." That's the tragedy. We've built a world where men can be collapsing internally while still mowing the lawn, holding down a job, and cracking jokes at parties. And then when they don't show up one day, we say we had no idea. But we did. We just weren't taught to see the signs. Or listen when they showed us without words.

Here's the part where I should say "there's hope." And there is. But it starts with something messier than optimism. It starts with unflinching honesty. With looking this crisis in the face and refusing to flinch. With building new language, new tools, new spaces where men can fall apart without losing their dignity. We need to dismantle the myth that asking for help is weak. That silence is strength. That dying quietly is better than living visibly. Because the truth is, most men don't want to die. They just don't see another way to stop hurting.

So what do we do? We start with this: we believe men when they say they're not okay. We stop pathologizing their silence and start translating it. We build mental health systems that meet men where they are—in their logic, their structure, their language. We train therapists who understand that emotional depth doesn't always look like tears. We teach boys early that vulnerability is not the opposite of strength—it's the foundation of it. We change how we talk about manhood in media, schools, locker rooms, and living rooms. We stop punishing men for breaking the mold we made too small for them to breathe inside.

And we grieve. For the ones who didn't make it. For the men we lost not to bullets or diseases, but to the slow strangling of their own humanity. We say their names. We stop pretending they were outliers. And we carry their stories forward—not as warnings, but as demands. That this stops here. That the next generation of men gets more than silence. Gets more than survival. Gets the language, the love, and the liberty to live fully.

Because the real epidemic isn't that men die by suicide.

It's that we still act surprised when they do.

CHAPTER 2

Addiction as Escape, Not Weakness

Men rarely walk into a therapist's office and say, "I'm hurting." They don't usually open with words like shame or emptiness. They don't volunteer childhood trauma on the first date, don't confess loneliness in the group chat, and they sure as hell don't sit down at a bar and say, "I'm in existential despair." What they do, though, is drink. Or gamble. Or scroll porn until their brain is a fried circuit of dopamine burnout and self-disgust. They overwork. Overtrain. Overeat. They play six hours of video games and call it unwinding. They edge toward risk with the kind of quiet desperation that doesn't look like a scream, but is. This chapter is about addiction—not the caricature, not the moral panic, but the reality. It's about how men in crisis don't always check into rehab or call suicide hotlines. Sometimes they just build lives around slowly numbing the pain. And the more socially acceptable the substance, the easier it is to pretend it's not killing them.

Addiction is often painted as pathology—as a failure of character, a broken brain, or a demon to be exorcised. But underneath the substance, underneath the behaviors, addiction is often something far more human: escape. Not from the world, but from the self. From shame. From buried grief. From pressure. From worthlessness. From boredom that feels like annihilation. According to the National Institute on Drug Abuse (NIDA), men are more likely than women to use almost all types of illicit drugs and are more likely to die from overdose. In fact, over 70% of opioid-related deaths in the U.S. are male. The reasons aren't random. They're baked into the way boys are raised, the way men are socialized, and the way pain gets metabolized in a male body conditioned to suppress, conceal, or convert emotion into distraction.

Let's start with alcohol—the great equalizer of male dysfunction. It's legal, accessible, and culturally encouraged. We call it "blowing off steam," "grabbing a cold one," "just having a few." But statistically, men binge drink at double the rate of women. The CDC defines binge drinking as five or more drinks in one sitting, and nearly a third of adult men admit to doing it regularly. The reality is far worse—because what men report and what men do often don't align. For many, alcohol isn't a treat—it's a sedative. A way to turn down the noise. To sleep. To feel something close to calm. Or to obliterate the feeling of not being enough, not being seen, not being able to hold it together another day. But because we've romanticized alcohol as masculine—a tool of celebration, rebellion, or emotional invulnerability—it often goes unchecked until it spirals. DUI. Domestic violence. Liver disease. Blackouts. Lost jobs. Broken families. But the drinking started long before the crash. It started the day no one asked why he was so quiet. The day he learned to smile through dread. The day he realized that whiskey doesn't talk back, judge, or leave.

And then there's porn. This one gets slippery, especially in a secular conversation, because moral panic tends to hijack the dialogue. But let's sidestep judgment and get honest. Pornography isn't inherently evil, but it is often used—excessively, compulsively, destructively—by men as anesthesia. It's easy. Free. Always available. No risk of rejection, no emotional labor, no vulnerability required. Just dopamine on demand. But over time, it can flatten the emotional range, distort expectations, and deepen a cycle of shame and avoidance. According to a 2023 meta-analysis from the Journal of Behavioral Addictions, excessive pornography use is strongly correlated with depression, anxiety, and interpersonal dysfunction in men—especially when it begins in adolescence and becomes the primary coping mechanism for stress, rejection, or boredom. It's not about lust. It's about loneliness. It's about the need for connection masquerading as arousal. And the deeper a man sinks into this pattern, the harder it becomes to reach out. Because now, his coping mechanism is wrapped in shame. And shame is the master key to silence.

We should also talk about work. Not the grind culture caricature, but the men who throw themselves into labor with the same intensity others throw into drugs. Overwork—whether in an office, a job site, or even creative hustle—is often a distraction from inner turmoil. It feels productive. It wins praise. It keeps the demons at bay. But it's still avoidance. The American Psychological Association found that men are less likely than women to take sick leave for mental health concerns, less likely to use vacation time, and more likely to associate self-worth with professional success. This is especially true among men in leadership positions, entrepreneurial roles, and high-pressure careers. They don't burn out because they love the job. They burn out because stopping would mean sitting with themselves. And that's scarier than death.

Of course, there's more traditional addiction—opioids, meth, cocaine, benzos—and men dominate every one of these categories in terms of abuse and overdose. But again, it's not about bad choices. It's about unprocessed pain. The National Institutes of Health report that men are more likely to self-medicate physical and psychological distress, and are less likely to access therapy, especially when that distress stems from trauma. Trauma, unspoken and untreated, becomes a parasite. And addiction is one of the few ways it knows how to feed. Men who've been abused, abandoned, rejected, or stripped of meaning often turn to substances not to chase a high—but to erase a low. Addiction is not euphoria. It's relief. Temporary. Damaging. But for many men, it feels like the only thing that works.

And then there's behavioral addiction. Gambling. Risk. Sex. Video games. Even fitness. The mechanism is the same: short-term stimulation to drown out long-term distress. Dopamine floods the system, giving the illusion of control, of power, of agency. But once the hit wears off, the pain is still there—and now it's wrapped in consequences. Financial ruin. Legal trouble. Broken trust. Or worse, a hollow sense that even the things that once brought relief no longer do. That's when despair calcifies. And that's where many men reach the most dangerous intersection: when the coping stops working, but the pain doesn't stop growing.

One of the cruelest aspects of male addiction is that it's often ignored or enabled until it's too late. Friends joke about the guy who drinks too much. "He's just blowing off steam." Families minimize the gambling. "He's got it under control." Workplaces reward overwork with promotions. "He's such a machine." Meanwhile, the man himself is drowning in plain sight. And because he's been trained not to ask for help, not to admit need, not to appear weak, he doubles down. He pushes harder. He isolates. He lies. Not out of malice—but because he believes, consciously or not, that no one would understand, that no one would forgive, that no one would help. And maybe, in some environments, he's not wrong.

So what do we do with all this? First, we redefine what addiction looks like in men. We stop waiting for the mugshot, the intervention, the overdose. We start recognizing addiction as any pattern of behavior used chronically to avoid pain at the cost of long-term wellbeing. That includes substances, yes. But also habits, rituals, and thought patterns. We have to stop asking, "What's wrong with you?" and start asking, "What happened to you?" Because addiction isn't about weakness. It's about wounds. Hidden ones. Old ones. Ones that never got permission to matter.

Second, we rebuild the conversation around support. Most addiction recovery models—especially faith-based ones—aren't built for secular men. They invoke surrender, moral inventory, divine intervention. But what if you don't believe in sin? What if God isn't part of the framework? That doesn't mean recovery is out of reach. It just means we need new models. Evidence-based, secular, shame-free approaches like CBT, DBT, harm reduction, somatic therapy, and trauma-informed care. We need rehab centers that don't require a higher power. We need group therapy that isn't just "cry or die." We need spaces where men can be logical and emotional, where structure isn't code for repression, and where healing doesn't require humiliation.

And we need to start younger. Early education around emotional literacy, stress management, and healthy coping isn't fluff—it's preventative care. Teach boys how to identify feelings before they become fists or habits. Model vulnerability in male role models. Let sons cry without punishing them with shame. Let fathers heal so they don't pass their pain down the line. Break the cycle not with slogans, but with tools.

Addiction, at its core, is the opposite of connection. That's why the solution isn't just sobriety—it's integration. Not abstaining, but reintegrating the parts of the self that have been exiled. The ashamed parts. The scared parts. The grieving parts. Men need more than discipline. They need compassion. They need accountability, yes—but also empathy. Not coddling. Not excuses. Just truth, shared in a way that doesn't alienate them further. Because the more we punish men for their addictions, the more they hide them. And the more they hide them, the more they spiral.

Here's what most people don't understand: men don't get addicted because they're reckless. They get addicted because it works—until it doesn't. And by the time it doesn't, they're already too deep, too ashamed, too isolated to climb out alone. That's where we come in. Not with lectures. Not with pity. But with language that says: you're not weak—you're wounded. And wounds can heal. Even this one.

Because no man was born addicted. He was born needing connection, safety, agency, and meaning. Take those things away, and he will build substitutes. They will feel good. They will stop the pain. Until they don't. And when that moment comes, when the bottom falls out, he won't need a sermon. He'll need a bridge. Built from science. Compassion. And the radical idea that healing is not about who you were—it's about who you get to become when the pain stops being a secret.

CHAPTER 3

The Cost of Stoicism

He doesn't cry at funerals. Doesn't flinch at pain. Doesn't talk about "feelings," except in half-sarcastic code. He shakes off heartbreak like a pulled muscle and wears exhaustion like a badge. He goes to work with migraines, hides panic attacks behind sarcasm, and clenches his jaw when life feels like it's folding in on him. His blood pressure is high, but he jokes it off. His sleep is garbage, but he powers through. His chest tightens some nights for no reason he can name, but he assumes it's just stress. And stress is normal, right? That's what being a man is—shouldering it all without complaint. Until it breaks him. Slowly, quietly, or catastrophically. This is the gospel of stoicism men are raised on, and this chapter is about the price tag it carries. Not the philosophical stoicism of Marcus Aurelius or modern-day resilience rhetoric. We're talking about the toxic, culturally embedded kind—the version that says the only way to be a man is to be unfazed, unfeeling, and unaffected. A statue with a bank account. And if you're not that, then you're either a failure or a fraud.

Let's get one thing straight right off the bat: the problem isn't stoicism itself. At its core, stoic philosophy—real stoic philosophy—is about grounding yourself in what you can control, accepting what you can't, and cultivating internal calm regardless of circumstance. That's healthy. That's maturity. But what most men inherit isn't philosophy. It's performance. A curated absence of emotion disguised as strength. A mask worn so long that it fuses to the skin. We tell boys not to cry. We tell men not to vent. We punish vulnerability, mock sensitivity, and reward emotional constipation with promotions and pats on the back.

Then we act surprised when those men implode, burn out, get sick, or disappear into addiction. Toxic stoicism doesn't make men strong—it makes them brittle. Unbreakable until they shatter.

There's a term for this phenomenon in psychological literature: normative male alexithymia—a socially conditioned difficulty in recognizing, naming, and expressing emotions. It's not a pathology. It's a pattern. It's what happens when a child is taught that only anger and pride are acceptable emotions, and everything else—fear, sadness, shame, guilt, grief—is a liability. Over time, the emotional vocabulary shrinks. Not just in speech, but in internal processing. The man doesn't know what he's feeling, because he was never taught the words. He doesn't recognize emotional escalation until it becomes a panic attack or a blow-up. He doesn't know how to comfort himself without distraction, doesn't know how to process loss without dissociation, doesn't know how to be known without performance. And beneath it all is an unspoken terror: What if someone sees the real me and walks away? So he buries it deeper. Powers through. And the body starts to carry what the mouth won't say.

This is where stoicism stops being a mindset and becomes a health risk. The American Psychological Association has long documented the mind-body connection in men—how repressed emotion doesn't just "go away," but instead finds refuge in the nervous system, cardiovascular system, and immune response. Chronic stress in men—especially unspoken, unprocessed emotional stress—leads to increased risk of hypertension, heart disease, obesity, ulcers, insomnia, and autoimmune dysfunction. According to the CDC, men are far more likely to die from preventable lifestyle diseases, and one of the key predictors isn't diet or exercise—it's stress management. Or rather, the lack of it. When emotions have no exit, they become poison. The body doesn't forget. It stores the panic, the grief, the shame, the fear. It tightens muscles, raises cortisol levels, disrupts sleep cycles, destabilizes hormones. And men, trained not to acknowledge any of this, normalize the decay. They call it "getting older." They say they're "fine." Meanwhile, their hearts are ticking time bombs.

And it's not just physical. The psychological cost is equally brutal. Toxic stoicism cuts men off from community. From their partners. From their kids. From themselves. It creates a version of masculinity that's functionally alone—even in a crowded room. Because you can't bond if you're always pretending you don't need anyone. You can't receive love if you've trained yourself to be unlovable. You can't share vulnerability if you've convinced yourself that it makes you pathetic. The stoic man is often admired, even respected. But inside, he's starving. For touch. For understanding. For someone to ask a second time when he says he's "alright." But because he wears the mask so well, no one does. And eventually, he forgets it's even a mask.

This stoic ideal also bleeds into how men show up in relationships—and often, how they fail in them. Emotional unavailability isn't just a personality quirk. It's a trauma response turned lifestyle. When a man hasn't been allowed to process emotion safely, he'll either detach or explode. And neither option fosters intimacy. Partners of emotionally suppressed men often describe feeling like they're in a relationship with a ghost. He's present, but not accessible. He's stable, but not safe to open up to. Or worse, he's critical, cold, or angry—because those are the only emotions he's allowed himself to express without fear of emasculation. The same walls that protect him from shame also block him from connection. And over time, those walls become prisons.

At work, the consequences look different—but they still cut deep. The stoic man often becomes hyper-functional, perfectionistic, and driven—but also burned out, brittle, and numb. He doesn't take breaks. Doesn't admit limits. Doesn't delegate. He overidentifies with his role, ties his self-worth to productivity, and treats rest like failure. And when burnout hits, he either grinds harder or spirals quietly. Employers love stoic men until they collapse. Then they're replaced. Because the machine doesn't reward humanity—it rewards output. And stoic men often don't realize until it's too late that they were disposable. Their emotional suppression didn't make them irreplaceable—it made them invisible.

The kicker? Most of this could be avoided if we stopped treating emotional expression like a feminine trait and started treating it like a human one. If we taught boys that crying isn't weakness—it's a pressure release. That anger is often grief in armor. That asking for help isn't surrender—it's intelligence. That feelings don't make you fragile—they make you functional. But we don't. We let locker rooms, media, and broken fathers raise boys into emotionally amputated men, then wonder why they crash and burn at 35, ghost their marriages at 40, and quietly give up at 50. We've created a model of manhood that's allergic to softness, allergic to nuance, allergic to need. And we call it strength. It's not.

There's a growing body of research that supports this. Studies from the University of British Columbia and Harvard Medical School confirm that men who score high on internalized masculine norms—especially emotional restriction—are significantly less likely to seek help for depression, anxiety, or trauma. They're also more likely to engage in maladaptive coping behaviors like substance abuse, risk-taking, and social withdrawal. This isn't about identity politics. It's about survival. The more rigid the emotional expectations, the more lethal the consequences.

And before someone jumps in with "but women suffer too"—yes, they do. This isn't a contest. It's a crisis. Men's mental health doesn't need to be more important than anyone else's to be urgent. It just needs to be real. And right now, we're still stuck in a culture where male suffering is either romanticized into silence (he's a lone wolf) or ridiculed into oblivion (man up). Neither helps. What helps is new language. New modeling. New spaces where emotional fluency isn't just allowed—it's expected.

So what's the alternative? Not open sobbing on Zoom calls or dumping trauma on first dates. Not performative vulnerability. Not "crying to go viral." Real emotional regulation. The ability to name what's going on beneath the surface. The courage to ask for help before you're on the brink. The skill to sit with hard feelings without numbing, lashing out, or shutting down. And most importantly, the belief that strength and sensitivity are not enemies—they're siblings. Real stoicism—the kind we should be teaching—isn't about denial. It's about discernment. About choosing when to speak, how to feel, and what to do next with honesty and integrity. That kind of stoicism doesn't kill men. It saves them.

But we don't get there by accident. We get there by breaking the cycle. By unlearning the myths. By teaching men, young and old, that the cost of stoicism isn't just missed connection—it's premature death. It's relationships that never go deep. It's kids who grow up not knowing how to talk to their fathers. It's lives that look "together" from the outside but feel hollow inside. And the only way to start healing is to give men the tools—and the permission—to feel again.

Because no man was born emotionless. No boy starts out stoic. The first thing every newborn does is scream. Then cry. Then reach. Then seek. Somewhere along the way, we told them to stop. To harden. To swallow it. But that's not manhood. That's self-erasure. And it's time we named it for what it is.

Stoicism isn't free. It comes at a cost. And men have been paying with their bodies, their relationships, and their lives. Enough.

CHAPTER 4

Fathers, Fight Clubs, and the Formation of Men

You don't become a man. You're built into one. Or you're not. That's the uncomfortable truth most cultures would rather spiritualize, romanticize, or deny. Boys don't simply hit a certain age and unlock manhood like a video game achievement—they absorb it, inherit it, stitch it into their bones from the people around them, the silences between words, and the rituals they don't even realize are rituals. And for far too many, what they inherit is absence. Not just in the literal sense—though that too—but in the emotional, spiritual, psychological sense. They inherit a blueprint for masculinity that's made of gaps. Gaps where tenderness should've been modeled. Gaps where fear should've been named. Gaps where love should've spoken louder than discipline. This chapter isn't about blaming dads or dunking on tradition. It's about exposing how the foundation of modern masculinity is often laid in broken soil: emotionally absent fathers, generational silence, and a culture that forces boys to prove their worth through violence, repression, or detachment long before they understand what any of it means.

Let's start with the most loaded figure in male development: the father. Or the absence of one. According to U.S. Census data, roughly 1 in 4 children grow up without a biological, step, or adoptive father in the home. For boys, that absence doesn't just create logistical hardship—it creates a psychic wound. One that festers quietly. Because even if a father is physically present, emotional absence leaves just as deep a scar. You can have a dad in the room who never looks you in the eyes. A provider who never teaches you how to process sadness. A disciplinarian who shows up for every game but never once says "I'm proud of you" unless there's a scoreboard. Boys learn early that love must be earned. That silence is safer. That validation is conditional. And many carry that unspoken equation into adulthood, wondering why they feel unworthy, invisible, or perpetually unsure of themselves even when life "looks fine." That confusion didn't start in college. It started when Dad never told them how to be.

Now compound that with intergenerational emotional illiteracy. Most fathers weren't taught to feel either. They were taught to provide. To protect. To push through. And in doing so, they passed down the same toolbox they were handed: mostly empty, save for a hammer made of anger and a measuring tape of success. Vulnerability wasn't modeled, it was mocked. Emotional nuance wasn't practiced, it was punished. And when they did hurt, these fathers—many of them well-meaning—simply shut down. They disappeared into work, alcohol, or the cold shell of patriarchal duty. Sons watched and learned. Not how to feel—but how to hide. Not how to process grief—but how to bury it under achievement or rage. What they didn't learn is that wounds unspoken become behaviors unexplained. Boys who aren't allowed to talk about their hurt grow into men who don't know how to love without conditions or exist without pressure.

And this isn't just anecdotal—it's clinical. The Adverse Childhood Experiences (ACE) study, one of the most significant public health studies in the last half-century, shows that childhood trauma—abuse, neglect, household dysfunction, abandonment—dramatically increases the risk of depression, substance use, heart disease, suicide, and premature death. Men with high ACE scores are far more likely to engage in high-risk behaviors and far less likely to seek help. But the trauma doesn't have to be dramatic to be damaging. Sometimes the absence is the trauma. A father who never says "I love you" is not legally abusive—but neurologically, it registers. A boy never comforted after failure may grow into a man who interprets every setback as a referendum on his worth. He becomes rigid, defensive, emotionally armored. Not out of malice. But because he was never taught another way.

Then come the cultural reinforcements. If the father wound doesn't seal a boy's emotional range shut, the wider world certainly tries. Schoolyards become battlegrounds where softness is punished and dominance is currency. Boys are taught to tease each other into conformity. To view compassion as weakness and aggression as strength. Vulnerability gets branded "gay," "soft," "pussy"—language loaded with homophobia, misogyny, and toxic survivalism. These aren't just insults. They're indoctrination tools. And the boys on the receiving end either learn to fight or learn to disappear. Both cost them their wholeness. The idea that a boy can be emotionally fluent and respected is still revolutionary in many circles. And by the time a young man enters adolescence, he's already learned to lie about what he feels. Not because he wants to—but because he's been trained to.

And what happens when that bottled confusion, sadness, and fear reach puberty? You get fight clubs. Not the literal kind—though sometimes yes, exactly that—but metaphorical ones too. Men test themselves, punish themselves, challenge each other to feats of toughness or sexual conquest or self-abuse. Hazing. Street fights. Reckless behavior. It's not about thrill. It's initiation. A desperate attempt to prove worth in a world that hasn't offered any other pathway. And for those who've had no loving father or elder male to guide them through this storm, masculinity becomes a hall of mirrors. Every version they try on feels hollow, performative, exhausting. But they don't know how to quit because quitting feels like failure. And the world has taught them that failure is death.

Even men who had "good dads" often inherit this framework. The dad may have been loving—but did he talk about emotion? Did he ever apologize? Did he show fear, cry in front of his children, model vulnerability, or admit mistakes? Or did he love quietly, work endlessly, and assume his presence was enough? Many men look back and say, "My dad was great, but we didn't really talk." That gap matters. Because boys don't learn emotional fluency by osmosis. They learn it through modeling. Through exposure. Through safe dialogue. Without it, they fill in the blanks with whatever the culture provides—and the culture is rarely healthy.

There's also a spiritual element here—not in the religious sense, but in the existential one. For centuries, manhood was marked by rituals—rites of passage that, while often problematic, at least acknowledged the transition from boy to man. Today, those rites are gone. Replaced by nothing. Boys wander into manhood without initiation, without mentorship, without direction. And in that vacuum, they grasp for anything that feels like structure: gym culture, YouTube gurus, toxic masculinity influencers who sell simplified masculinity in three easy steps—dominate, detach, defend. And because these voices are often the only ones speaking directly to their pain, young men listen. Not because they're hateful—but because they're lost. And bad maps are better than no maps at all.

If we want to change the future of men's mental health, we have to start where it begins. In the home. In the language we use with boys. In how we train fathers—not just to provide, but to emotionally parent. We need to teach dads that saying "I love you" every day is not excessive. That apologizing when you're wrong is strength, not surrender. That playing catch is good, but asking your son how he's feeling is better. We need schools that teach emotional regulation as seriously as math. We need coaches who don't scream shame but build character. We need friends who challenge each other with "how are you really?" instead of "you good?" We need to break the chain.

And we need secular male role models who don't lean on religious language or patriarchal structures to define manhood. We need men who show up whole. Who are successful and sensitive. Who are strong and soft. Who cry without shame and fight only when they have to—and even then, with restraint. We need to teach young men that their value isn't in domination, conquest, stoicism, or silence—but in honesty, compassion, accountability, and emotional courage. That being a man is not about what you hide, but about what you heal.

Because here's the hardest truth: many of the men struggling today aren't broken. They were just built by broken blueprints. And no one ever gave them permission to rebuild. So they walk through life thinking their anxiety is weakness. That their depression is failure. That their loneliness is deserved. They become fathers with no map, partners with no language, workers with no sense of self beyond the next paycheck. And unless someone interrupts that cycle—unless we offer them new tools—they will pass the same emotional poverty down to the next generation.

We cannot fix the mental health crisis among men without healing the early formation of boys. That means rethinking how we talk to them, how we guide them, and how we support their growth into men who feel whole, seen, and safe. Not coddled. Not fragile. Just human. Fully human. And no, not every man's pain traces back to dad. But many do. And even more trace back to a world that refused to acknowledge how deep those wounds went.

We were told to be strong. But nobody told us how.

Now it's our job to learn—and then teach the next generation something better.

CHAPTER 5

The Alpha Lie: Modern Masculinity in Ruins

They told you to be an alpha. To dominate, not discuss. To lead without asking, take without apologizing, and conquer every room you walk into like the laws of nature demand it. They called it confidence, but really, it was a costume. A performance rooted not in strength but fear. The "alpha male" myth has sold itself so well that even the men it's killing think it's keeping them alive. But here's the truth most of them never got the memo on: there's no such thing as an alpha male. Not in science. Not in society. Not in reality. The term was built on a misreading of wolf behavior in the 1940s that's been debunked for decades, yet it still claws at men's identities like gospel. Why? Because it offers simple answers to complex pain. Because it speaks to the boy who never felt enough, never felt seen, and needed a role to play that would finally silence the voice in his head saying he was nothing. This chapter is a dismantling of that mythology. Because until men are freed from the prison of false masculinity, they'll keep measuring themselves against a ghost—and bleeding for it.

The modern alpha lie is a Frankenstein monster of outdated Darwinian logic, locker room bravado, pop psychology, and Instagram hustle culture. It tells men their worth is found in power, dominance, sexual conquest, status, and emotional detachment. That vulnerability is a liability. That nuance is weakness. That other men are rivals, not brothers. And that any failure—financial, romantic, physical—is a mark of inferiority. But what's most insidious about this myth is not just that it's fake. It's that it's marketable. Entire ecosystems profit off men feeling inadequate and offering the alpha fantasy as salvation.

The manosphere—an unholy cocktail of red-pill forums, YouTube influencers, and grift-laced masculinity coaches—peddles this vision of manhood to millions of young men desperately trying to make sense of themselves in a world that no longer hands them clear rites of passage. And the content works. It's intoxicating. It tells men what they want to hear: that the reason they're failing isn't their fault—it's women, weak men, feminists, modernity, softness, emotion, politics, society. Everyone else. The cure? Be harder. Be colder. Be alpha. The result? A generation of emotionally stunted, socially isolated men who mistake contempt for confidence and loneliness for leadership.

But masculinity isn't monolithic. It never was. The idea that there's one "real" way to be a man has always been a cultural invention, reshaped with every era, every empire, every ideology. The Spartans had one version. The Victorians had another. Capitalism remixed it. Religion weaponized it. Hollywood romanticized it. And now the algorithm monetizes it. But none of it is inherently true. It's all just stories we tell ourselves—stories that often leave men trapped in roles they never chose, performing toughness they don't feel, chasing success they don't want, and repressing emotions that are eating them alive. And the harder they try to be "alpha," the more disconnected they become from themselves, their relationships, and the kind of meaning that can't be bought or bullied into existence.

Let's look at the science for a second. The term "alpha male" was first coined by animal behaviorist Rudolph Schenkel, who observed dominance hierarchies in captive wolves. But those wolves were in cages—stressed, aggressive, and unnatural. Later research, especially by David Mech, revealed that in wild packs, the "alpha" dynamic doesn't exist the way we thought. Wolf packs are family units. The leaders are simply parents. Not dominators. Not tyrants. Just caregivers. Mech himself has spent decades trying to correct the public's misunderstanding of his early work. But the myth had already taken root—first in pop culture, then in male self-help spaces, and now across the internet like a virus. It's ironic: the very science used to justify modern masculinity rejects the conclusion entirely. But truth doesn't sell. Insecurity does.

And insecurity is the fuel. Underneath every alpha act is fear—of irrelevance, weakness, invisibility. A man who needs to dominate others to feel okay with himself is not strong. He's starving. Starving for identity, for purpose, for approval, for the father figure who never told him he was enough without the flex. This is why the alpha myth doesn't just attract sociopaths—it attracts the scared. And once inside, it gives them tools to bury their fear instead of facing it. But buried fear doesn't go away. It just shows up elsewhere: in broken relationships, emotional abuse, arrested development, performative bravado, and eventually, isolation. Because the alpha doesn't ask for help. Doesn't connect. Doesn't grow. He just postures. And then wonders why no one loves him for who he really is.

We also need to talk about how this myth creates enemies out of potential allies. The alpha script demands constant competition. With other men. With women. With the world. There's no room for tenderness, for collaboration, for emotional reciprocity. It's all conquest. And in this worldview, women become either prizes to be won or threats to be neutralized. Emotional men become weaklings. Queer men become jokes. Vulnerable men become targets. The result is a masculine culture so hostile that many men have no safe place to just be. Not in friend groups. Not in relationships. Not even alone—because the internal critic becomes just as ruthless as the external culture. And so men harden, isolate, numb, and eventually collapse. Not because they're weak. But because they've been following a script that was never built to end well.

And that collapse often looks like burnout, loneliness, failed intimacy, addiction, or quiet resignation. The alpha myth tells men they're only valuable if they're winning. But life is not constant victory. Everyone loses sometimes. Everyone fails. Everyone ages. Everyone breaks. So what happens to the man whose identity was built on dominance when he gets laid off, gets dumped, gets sick, or just gets tired? He falls apart. Because he was never allowed to be human—only heroic. And heroes don't rest. They don't cry. They don't grieve. They die. The world doesn't need more dying heroes. It needs more living, breathing, feeling, flawed, evolving men.

So what's the alternative? Adaptive masculinity. Not a retreat into fragility, but a progression into wholeness. Adaptive masculinity says you can be strong and soft. Assertive and collaborative. Driven and present. It embraces emotional fluency, rejects binary thinking, and values men not for their dominance but their depth. It creates space for multiple expressions of manhood—fatherhood, brotherhood, mentorship, vulnerability, creativity, accountability. It doesn't fear women's empowerment. It doesn't mock therapy. It doesn't punch down to feel tall. It's rooted in self-awareness, not status. In resilience, not repression.

We also need to reclaim masculinity from the grifters. From the influencers who sell misogyny as confidence and peddle emotional numbness as empowerment. These men are not leaders. They are merchants of insecurity. Parasites feeding on the fear of young men who were never given better maps. The rise of figures like Andrew Tate isn't an accident—it's a vacuum. And unless we fill that vacuum with something better, more grounded, more honest, more humane, the next generation will keep falling into the same pit. Not because they're evil. But because they're looking for a place to belong—and all they're finding is war.

Belonging is the key. Because at its heart, the alpha myth is about exclusion. You're either top dog or nobody. And that's a recipe for widespread despair. We need communities where men can show up messy, confused, in-progress—and still be loved. We need peer groups that prize curiosity over certainty. We need role models who talk about failure with grace and success without ego. We need men who model being over dominating. And we need to raise boys who know that real strength isn't how many people you can beat—but how many people you can lift.

Because the truth is, men are not predators by nature. They're adaptable. Capable of immense tenderness, loyalty, empathy, and care. We see it in fathers who change diapers at 3 a.m. We see it in brothers who show up for each other during loss. We see it in friendships that survive decades. In mentors who listen. In partners who hold space instead of holding power. That's masculinity too. And it's time we stop pretending it's optional or secondary.

The alpha lie doesn't just hurt men. It isolates them. It robs them of joy, of depth, of real connection. It teaches them to fear softness, to reject reflection, to perform constantly. And for what? Approval from strangers? Validation from other wounded men playing the same hollow game? That's not power. That's a cage. And too many men are dying inside it—emotionally, spiritually, sometimes literally. We don't need more posturing. We need permission. To be real. To be raw. To be free.

So here's the new script: You don't have to be alpha. You don't have to win every room. You don't have to crush the competition. You don't have to seduce, dominate, outperform, or out-tough your way into manhood. You're already enough. Not because of what you conquer, but because of what you carry—and how you carry it. You're allowed to hurt. You're allowed to rest. You're allowed to feel. You're allowed to rewrite your story. And you're allowed to step off the stage, drop the act, and become someone real.

Because when the myth dies, the man can finally live.

CHAPTER 6

No Tribe, No God, No Net

Most men don't implode in a blaze of obvious tragedy. They disappear by degrees. One missed call. One canceled plan. One weekend with no plans at all. Then it's months. Then it's years. No tribe. No god. No net. And by the time anyone notices how far they've drifted, the man in question doesn't recognize himself anymore—not the boy he was, not the man he was supposed to become, and certainly not the ghost he's quietly morphed into. This chapter is about that drifting. That emotional vanishing act. That quiet plague of isolation that wraps around men like a weighted blanket and slowly strangles their will to connect, to feel, to live. And it's not just sad—it's lethal. Because as much as we like to preach independence, the truth is this: humans don't do well alone. Men especially. The myth of the lone wolf sounds noble until you realize wolves die without a pack. This is the cost of modern male isolation. And it's happening faster, deeper, and more dangerously than most are willing to admit.

Let's talk numbers. The 2023 U.S. Surgeon General's Advisory on the epidemic of loneliness and isolation reported that lacking social connection can increase the risk of premature death by over 60%, rivaling the health risks of smoking 15 cigarettes a day. That's not hyperbole. That's science. And it's not just a global crisis—it's a gendered one. According to studies by the American Perspectives Survey and Pew Research, men report fewer close friendships than women, are significantly less likely to reach out when struggling, and often lose their last meaningful social ties by middle age. The average American man today is lonelier, more disconnected, and more emotionally isolated than at any point in recorded history. And yet, culture still treats this as an individual problem—something to be solved with grit, gym memberships, or a side hustle. But this isn't about willpower. It's about wiring. We were not built to suffer in solitude. And yet, that's exactly what we keep asking men to do.

Religion, for all its baggage, used to serve as a social anchor for many men. It offered ritual, community, accountability, and at least some semblance of shared meaning. But as religiosity declines—especially among younger men—those old support structures are vanishing, and nothing has taken their place. According to Pew Research Center data, nearly 40% of men under 30 now identify as religiously unaffiliated. That's not a moral failure. That's a sociological shift. But the result is the same: men who walk away from churches, temples, and mosques often walk away from their last stable form of weekly human connection. And they don't know where else to go. Women, historically, build social support laterally—friendships, circles, community-based bonds. But men, especially those raised with stoic expectations and competitive models of masculinity, often tie their identity vertically—to work, marriage, or organized systems like religion. So when those systems crumble, the scaffolding collapses. And what's left isn't freedom. It's free fall.

But loneliness for men isn't always visible. That's the trick. It doesn't look like crying on a park bench. It looks like endless hours of gaming. It looks like working late every night. It looks like porn tabs and empty fridges and takeout containers stacking on the floor. It looks like "I've just been busy." Like "I'm good, just tired." It looks like a man who used to be the loudest laugh in the group chat and now leaves every message on read. Like a guy who cancels dinner because he "forgot" but really, he just couldn't get out of bed. Loneliness in men wears masks. It borrows the face of functionality. It slips under the radar until it metastasizes into something harder to name: apathy, burnout, bitterness, anger, hopelessness. And eventually, it sinks its teeth into the very question of worth: Why try? Who would even notice if I stopped showing up?

This isn't weakness. This is a human in deficit. Starved for connection in a world that keeps telling him connection is optional—or worse, embarrassing. Think about how few spaces exist for men to be fully seen without performing. It's not the bar. It's not the gym. It's not the workplace. Therapy is stigmatized. Group chats are surface-level. And the moment a man expresses deep vulnerability, most people freeze—because we've collectively been conditioned to see male sadness as either suspicious or pathetic. So the man learns not to share. Not because he doesn't want to—but because he's been punished every time he did. He tried being honest. Someone laughed. Or changed the subject. Or weaponized his pain later. That lesson calcifies. And over time, he stops reaching out. Not because he's healed—but because he's trained.

Even romantic relationships, for many men, are no longer safe harbors. As gender roles evolve and emotional expectations increase, many men enter relationships ill-equipped for mutual vulnerability. They've never had the reps. Never had a model. They don't know how to express what they feel without sounding angry. They don't know how to hold space for a partner's pain without retreating or reacting. So they shut down. They disappoint. They fail to meet needs they were never taught to understand. And when those relationships fall apart—especially in middle age—their final support beam crumbles. Divorced men face some of the highest rates of suicide and depression in the industrialized world. Not because they lost a spouse. But because they lost their last emotional translator. And now, there's no one left to help them speak human.

The secular man, in particular, is at a crossroads. Without a religious net to catch him, without inherited rituals to mark transitions, without a tribe to carry his burdens, he floats. Untethered. Many want meaning but don't believe in a god. They want connection but don't know where to find it that doesn't feel like forced intimacy or shallow networking. They want brotherhood, but the modern world offers few models for male closeness that aren't coded as weakness or wrapped in irony. The result is existential loneliness—a kind of disconnection not just from people, but from purpose. And in that void, it's no wonder so many men grab onto anything that offers even the illusion of structure: toxic ideologies, parasocial online relationships, self-improvement cults, digital rabbit holes that promise belonging but deliver addiction. Because any community, even a bad one, feels better than none at all.

So what do we do about this? First, we stop pretending that men can self-rescue from loneliness. That's like asking someone to pull themselves out of a pit they don't know they've fallen into. Connection has to be modeled, initiated, nurtured. Not by demanding emotional vulnerability from men who've been punished for it their whole lives, but by offering consistent presence, nonjudgmental spaces, and alternatives to isolation that don't feel like charity or punishment. We need to normalize male friendship—not the performative, shoulder-punching kind, but the real kind. Conversations without agendas. Affection without mockery. Loyalty without conditions. We need to dismantle the idea that intimacy is only romantic and that the only acceptable male bond is war.

Second, we need to replace lost ritual with new ones. Not religious, necessarily—but rhythmic. Spaces where men can show up, connect, and be seen regularly. Whether it's men's groups, therapy circles, creative workshops, hobby-based communities, or even secular ceremonies that mark transitions—these structures matter. The human brain is built for pattern and story. When you strip those away, you don't get freedom—you get drift. Especially in men, who've been raised to see purpose as external, status-driven, and measurable. New models of meaning have to be offered. Otherwise, they'll keep retreating into silence, into consumption, into numbness.

We also need to stop penalizing male loneliness with ridicule. Every time someone mocks a lonely man, another one withdraws. Every time a man is shamed for trying to reconnect—be it with his kids, his emotions, his friends, his health—we reinforce the idea that his needs are pathetic. We need to build a world where men can re-enter without humiliation. Where healing doesn't require an apology. Where being "soft" is not an insult but a sign that maybe, just maybe, you've stopped pretending.

And finally, we need to name the pain. Not all men are lonely. But far too many are, and even more are afraid to admit it. Because loneliness sounds like failure. Like loser talk. But it's not. It's human. It's common. And it's curable—not through grind, not through games, not through guru-led retreats, but through real connection, mutual recognition, and the slow, uncomfortable, beautiful work of rebuilding community from the ground up.

Men are not meant to go it alone. But many do. And it's killing them—not just in body, but in soul. It doesn't have to be that way.

Let's give them a net. A tribe. A way back to each other.

Before they vanish for good.

CHAPTER 7

Anger Is Grief in Armor

He yells at traffic like it personally insulted him. He punches walls when no one's looking. He slams the door a little too hard, raises his voice when he's scared, and calls it "just venting." At work, he's short-tempered. At home, he's distant until he explodes. With friends, he's the guy who snaps over nothing, then apologizes like nothing happened. Sometimes, he doesn't even realize he's angry—he just feels off, irritable, impatient, perpetually on edge. Anger becomes his language because it's the only emotion he was never punished for speaking. But what nobody tells him—and what most people around him never understand—is that the anger isn't the problem. It's the disguise. The smoke. The armor. Underneath, there's grief. Sadness. Shame. Fear. Confusion. But those got locked away a long time ago, and all that's left now is heat. This chapter is about that heat. About how anger becomes the only way many men know how to express pain. And how that makes them dangerous—not to the world, necessarily—but to themselves.

Culturally, we've given men exactly one acceptable emotional outlet: rage. Sadness? Weak. Fear? Cowardly. Anxiety? Just "man up." But fury? That's allowed. In fact, in many environments, it's rewarded. Anger is treated like strength—like the raw material of leadership, assertiveness, confidence. But real anger—the kind that shows up out of nowhere, the kind that hijacks the nervous system, the kind that destroys relationships and corrodes self-worth—isn't power. It's panic in armor. It's grief with no map. And most men have no idea it's even happening because they've never been taught to connect the dots between their explosions and their pain. They just know they feel like they're going to burst. And then they do. And then they hate themselves for it.

Psychologically, anger is what's known as a secondary emotion. It often arrives to mask a more vulnerable feeling underneath. Hurt. Embarrassment. Betrayal. Powerlessness. But if you're never given permission to name those things, you'll default to the one that doesn't get you laughed at or punished. Boys learn this early. Fall down and cry? You're a baby. Get teased and cry? You're soft. Get betrayed and cry? Toughen up. But get mad? Ah. Now you're strong. Now you're standing up for yourself. Now you're masculine. And so, anger becomes the default emotional interface. The only safe channel. And the older a boy gets, the more that channel calcifies until even he believes that's all there is. He doesn't feel sad. He's just pissed off. Doesn't feel ashamed—just annoyed. Doesn't feel lonely—just "tired of people's bullshit." He doesn't realize he's grieving because no one ever told him that grief doesn't always look like tears. Sometimes, it looks like clenched fists, tight jaws, and irrational outbursts over trivial things.

But here's where it gets more dangerous: when men start believing that their anger is their personality. They say things like "I just have a short fuse," or "It's just how I am." And society mostly lets them. We let men fume and snap and dominate conversations. We let them bully their way through feelings they don't understand. But we don't ask why they're like that. We don't ask what they're trying not to feel. And if we do, they don't have the vocabulary to answer. Because what would it mean to say out loud: "I'm not mad. I'm mourning. I'm scared. I'm ashamed. I'm hurting, and I don't know how to stop"? For most men, that level of honesty is unthinkable. Too vulnerable. Too raw. Too close to exposure. So instead, they armor up. And that armor becomes identity. Until it breaks them.

Let's talk about what that armor costs. Anger held over time rewires the brain. Chronic stress, heightened cortisol, an overactive amygdala—all of it wears the nervous system down. Anger floods the body with stress hormones that, over time, lead to increased risk of heart disease, high blood pressure, insomnia, digestive issues, and stroke. The American Psychological Association has repeatedly confirmed that unresolved anger is a major contributor to long-term physical health decline—especially in men who suppress all other emotional outlets. And because anger is so often normalized in male spaces—especially in competitive work environments, sports, and hyper-masculine subcultures—it doesn't get treated as a warning sign. It gets dismissed. "He's just intense." "He's just got a temper." "He's just passionate." But the body knows better. The body keeps score. And eventually, that score settles with interest.

It also destroys relationships. Anger is isolating. It creates an emotional minefield that partners, children, coworkers, and friends learn to tiptoe around. People stop being honest with angry men. They stop feeling safe. They withhold. They retreat. And the angry man, already disconnected from his own emotional truth, senses the distance but interprets it as rejection. So he lashes out more. Tries to regain control. Pushes people away with the very emotion he thinks will make them stay. And deep down, he hates himself for it. Not because he's cruel—but because he doesn't know another way to protect the boy inside him who never learned how to feel without burning.

We also need to confront how often male anger gets misdiagnosed—or completely missed—by mental health professionals. Male depression doesn't always look like sadness. It looks like irritation. Restlessness. Risk-taking. Substance abuse. Rage. But because the diagnostic criteria for depression were largely developed based on female presentations—crying, hopelessness, withdrawal—many men fly under the radar. They don't show up in clinics saying "I feel depressed." They show up after a DUI. After a fight. After a breakup. After they punched a hole in the wall. And by then, the shame has usually doubled down into denial. They don't feel safe admitting they're struggling. They feel cornered. And the moment you use words like "emotional vulnerability," they shut down. Not because they're incapable—but because they've never heard those words without judgment attached. Never experienced those states without fear. So they say they're fine. They're just tired. Just stressed. Just pissed. And everyone lets that be enough—until it's not.

So what do we do? First, we stop treating male anger like a personality trait and start treating it like a symptom. Not in a patronizing way. Not in a "let's calm you down, big guy" way. But in a clinical, human, intelligent way. We ask what's underneath. We build trust. We help men decode their own emotional lives by giving them language that doesn't feel condescending or foreign. We show them that anger is not the enemy—but the signal. A flare from deeper pain. Something that, when understood, can be redirected into clarity, action, healing. But left unchecked, will eat them alive and burn everyone close in the process.

Second, we normalize men talking about what hurts before it becomes rage. Not just in therapy, but in friendships, families, public conversations. That means showing boys and men what healthy emotional regulation looks like. Modeling it. Naming it. It means telling a ten-year-old boy that it's okay to cry and explaining why he's sad. It means telling a teenager that grief doesn't make him soft. It means telling a 40-year-old man that he's allowed to miss his father, to hate himself some days, to be scared about money, and that none of that makes him any less of a man. It means giving men context for their pain—not just consequences.

We also need to separate anger from abuse—because while anger itself is not evil, how it's expressed absolutely matters. This isn't a get-out-of-jail-free card for violence, manipulation, or cruelty. Being hurt doesn't justify hurting others. But shaming the expression of anger altogether only drives it deeper underground, where it festers. What men need are tools—not just lectures. Tools to pause, to reflect, to regulate. Tools to ask themselves, "What am I really feeling right now?" before they erupt. Tools to say, "I'm not okay, and I need help," without choking on the words.

There's also a philosophical truth here that men, especially those who have left religion behind, need to rediscover: that grief is not failure. It's evidence of care. Of love. Of presence. Men grieve all the time, but no one calls it that. We don't call it grief when a man retires and loses his sense of identity. When a father watches his kids grow up and feels purposeless. When a man loses a friend to suicide but doesn't know how to cry. When a breakup sends him spiraling but he pretends it didn't matter. That's grief. And if we called it what it is, maybe more men would stop masking it with anger and start moving through it with dignity.

Because at the end of the day, men don't want to be angry. Not really. Not the way we've been led to believe. The outbursts, the resentment, the cold silences—none of it feels good. It feels out of control. It feels shameful. And for many, it's followed by days of self-loathing, regret, and deeper isolation. Anger doesn't solve the problem—it just delays the inevitable. Eventually, the grief will surface. The question is whether the man will have the tools and the space to face it—or whether he'll keep armoring up until there's nothing left underneath but exhaustion.

So here's the truth: the angriest man in the room is almost always the saddest. The most violent outburst usually has the most frightened heart behind it. And the man who tells you he's fine but looks like he's about to boil over? He's not fine. He's fractured. Not broken beyond repair—but fraying. And what he needs is not another warning to "calm down." What he needs is someone—anyone—to say: "You don't have to carry it like this. There's another way."

Because anger, when named, can become clarity.

When understood, it can become strength.

When released, it can become healing.

But when ignored?

It becomes the fuse to everything a man loves burning down around him.

CHAPTER 8

The Body Remembers What the Mind Denies

He's exhausted, but he can't sleep. He wakes up sore, wired, angry for no reason. His back aches. His stomach churns. His jaw stays clenched until it pulses like a drumbeat behind his eyes. He shrugs it off—blames stress, bad posture, whatever he ate last night. Maybe he hits the gym harder. Maybe he ignores it and drowns it in caffeine, noise, porn, work. But the symptoms keep coming. Fatigue. Chest tightness. Shallow breathing. A strange hollowness that no nap or night out ever seems to fix. His doctor finds nothing wrong. Bloodwork's clean. "Try relaxing," they say. "Cut back on stress." As if he didn't already know that. What no one tells him—what few even think to ask—is whether his body is carrying the weight of everything he's never said. Whether his gut aches because his heart's been armored too long. Whether his chronic tension isn't bad luck or bad habits—but unspoken trauma making a home in his muscles. This chapter is about that body. The one that holds what the man refuses to feel. It's about how male pain goes somatic—not because they're weak, but because they've been denied the vocabulary, the rituals, and the support to process their emotional lives. Their minds won't name the grief—but their bodies remember everything.

Let's start with the hard science. The field of psychoneuroimmunology—the study of how psychological stress impacts the immune, nervous, and endocrine systems—has long confirmed what most men only realize too late: chronic emotional suppression causes physical damage. Long-term stress floods the body with cortisol and adrenaline, disrupting everything from digestion to hormone regulation to sleep cycles. Depression in men is frequently misdiagnosed as insomnia, muscle pain, digestive issues, or persistent fatigue. Why? Because instead of sadness, they report body complaints. They don't say, "I feel empty." They say, "I feel off." They don't say, "I'm grieving." They say, "I've been getting headaches." And because doctors are trained to look for what they can measure, they often miss what they can't see: emotional pain metastasizing through the nervous system like an invisible poison.

GI issues in men, for example, are massively underdiscussed in mental health circles. IBS, bloating, acid reflux, chronic indigestion—many of these have links not just to diet, but to stress and anxiety. The gut is often called the "second brain" for a reason: it's lined with millions of neurons and is directly connected to the brain via the vagus nerve. Emotional distress often shows up there first. It's no coincidence that men who say they have "gut problems" often report high levels of unresolved anger, grief, or dread. But again, few make the connection—because no one taught them how to link emotion and biology. They treat the symptom, not the source. More Tums, more caffeine, more pushing through. And the body keeps the score.

Pain is another common disguise. Chronic neck tension. Migraines. Joint stiffness. Muscle soreness that doesn't match activity. These are not just orthopedic issues—they're often emotional symptoms that have calcified in the body. Men raised in stoic cultures, those who grew up with abusive or emotionally absent parents, or those who've endured long-term relationship stress, often carry their pain in physical form because expressing it verbally feels unsafe or foreign. You'll hear them say, "I don't know what's wrong—I just feel tense all the time." That's not coincidence. That's an alarm. The trauma didn't go away. It just found a quieter place to live.

And then there's sleep—the first thing to go when the nervous system is on fire. Men with unresolved emotional trauma often experience insomnia, shallow sleep, early waking, or restless tossing that leaves them drained no matter how long they lie in bed. The body can't relax because the brain has flagged the system as unsafe. Even in rest, the alert remains. This is especially true for men with high-functioning anxiety—those who seem productive and successful on the outside, but are internally riddled with doubt, hypervigilance, and fear of collapse. Their bodies never feel safe enough to let go. So they exist in a state of constant, quiet tension. Until the body gives out—either slowly, through burnout and illness, or suddenly, through breakdown.

But perhaps the most overlooked somatic symptom in men is numbness—not just emotional detachment, but actual sensory dullness. Lack of appetite. Low libido. Diminished physical pleasure. Men may lose the ability to enjoy things—food, sex, touch, laughter—because their bodies have shifted into conservation mode. When the nervous system is under threat long enough, it stops prioritizing pleasure and focuses entirely on survival. Men don't talk about this because they don't know what it means. They assume they're broken. They blame age. They bury it. But numbness is not the absence of pain—it's the aftermath of too much of it.

So why don't men talk about these symptoms? Because they've been trained not to link their bodies to their emotions. They've been taught to see themselves as machines: input work, output results. If the machine breaks, fix it quickly. Don't ask why it's breaking. Don't look under the hood. Just duct tape it and keep moving. This model works—until it doesn't. Until the panic attacks start. Until the sleep disappears. Until the body stops cooperating, and the man is left wondering how a life that "looked fine" fell apart from the inside out. The answer is simple and brutal: what the mind can't say, the body screams.

We also need to talk about trauma. Not just the big, obvious kinds—assault, war, disaster—but the chronic, unspoken kinds that men endure without acknowledgment. Emotional neglect. Rejection. Performance pressure. Social invisibility. Father wounds. Cultural invalidation. These experiences often never get named as trauma, but they are. And the body doesn't distinguish between big T trauma and little t trauma—it just knows something isn't right. Somatic trauma therapy is beginning to gain traction for this reason—it recognizes that trauma is not just a memory but a pattern, locked into the nervous system and repeated daily through posture, breath, tension, avoidance, and behavior. Men carry these patterns silently. They clench their jaws instead of crying. They hold their breath instead of speaking up. They hunch inward, fists clenched, eyes down, hearts armored. Not because they're cowards. But because their body learned it wasn't safe to be open.

The secular man is especially at risk for internalizing trauma somatically. Without the language of confession, the ritual of surrender, or the communal acknowledgment of pain that some religious systems offer, many men have nowhere to place their burdens. There's no priest. No circle. No tradition to contain the chaos. So they stuff it. Deep. Into bone and breath and skin. And when it finally leaks out, it's misdiagnosed as disinterest, dysfunction, or disease. But the soul—however you define it—never forgets. Even if you don't believe in one, your nervous system has a memory longer than any journal, and it remembers the heartbreak you never grieved, the betrayal you never voiced, the childhood loss you never spoke of. That's what the body holds. That's what it's trying to process every time it spasms, flinches, tightens, or shuts down.

So what do we do? First, we change the way we talk about health. Men need to be taught—early, clearly, and consistently—that emotional health is physical health. That tight shoulders might be sadness. That stomach pain might be anxiety. That chronic fatigue might be repressed grief. We need doctors who ask not just what hurts, but why now? What's changed? What are you carrying? What haven't you said out loud? We need therapists who recognize somatic symptoms as valid entry points, not distractions. We need partners and friends who notice tension and ask, "What's going on in your world?" instead of assuming it's just "a long week."

Second, we need tools. Breathwork, somatic experiencing, EMDR, trauma-informed yoga, massage, guided body scans—these aren't New Age fluff. They're evidence-based practices that allow men to reconnect with the body they've been trained to ignore. Not every man needs to become a meditator. But every man deserves a nervous system that doesn't think he's in danger 24/7. And if that means learning to breathe deeper, to stretch in silence, to name where in his body he feels fear—then that's what healing looks like. Not just for his mind, but for his actual survival.

We also need to reclaim emotional language in male spaces. Men need to be able to say "My back hurts because I'm carrying too much" and have it mean more than physical weight. To say "I'm tired" and have someone understand that it's not just sleep—they're soul-tired. Life-tired. They need permission to interpret their symptoms not just as mechanical failures but emotional signals. And they need that permission from other men. Not just therapists. Not just partners. Brothers. Friends. Coworkers. Communities where the words "What's your body telling you?" aren't weird—they're normal.

Because the body isn't just flesh. It's history. It's memory. It's a record of everything the man never dared to say out loud. Every slammed door. Every time he said "I'm fine" when he was screaming inside. Every time he stuffed grief under productivity, or swallowed rage with a smile. The body holds it. And until that man is given the tools, the space, and the permission to release it—he will keep paying the price. In sleep. In sickness. In sadness that has no name but screams through his nerves anyway.

You can't think your way out of a body that's under siege.

You have to listen.

You have to move.

You have to feel.

Because if the mind won't tell the truth, the body will.

And eventually—it'll stop asking nicely.

CHAPTER 9

Numb, Dumb, and Gone: Disappearing Men

Not every man dies by suicide. Some just stop showing up. To birthdays. To relationships. To themselves. They go silent, flat, emotionally vacant. They quit the team, miss the calls, drift out of friend groups without fanfare or fallout. They stop laughing. Stop initiating. Stop dreaming. They work, maybe. They nod along. They say "I'm good" on autopilot. But there's a vacancy behind the eyes, a flatness in the voice, a hollowness in the laugh that no one can quite name, so most don't ask. Because it's easier to accept the shell than confront what's missing. This is the quiet disappearance of men. Not always physical. Not always dramatic. But real. Profound. Widespread. This chapter is about that erosion—the slow, invisible bleed of selfhood that happens when men, overwhelmed and unsupported, go emotionally offline. It's what happens when numbness wins. When exhaustion outpaces hope. When men don't blow up—they fade out. They ghost life. And no one notices until they're gone in every way that counts.

The warning signs don't look like we think they should. Disappearing men don't always send red flags. They function. They show up to work. They pay bills. They post memes. But their passions vanish. Their routines fray. Their eye contact slips. They're less present in conversations. Their hobbies collect dust. They don't rage—they recede. They don't cry—they shut down. And they rationalize it as being tired, being busy, being fine. But what's really happening is psychic frostbite. The emotional nervous system has gone numb from too much unspeakable strain. Too much chronic invalidation. Too much weight with nowhere to set it down. And in that frozen interior, the man simply stops reaching out. Not because he doesn't want help. But because he no longer believes help is real.

And why would he? Look around. In a culture that still jokes about male suffering, that still mocks emotion in men as weakness, that still treats exhaustion like a badge of honor and disconnection like stoicism, it makes perfect sense that many men eventually opt out—not with pills or ropes, but with silence. With slow disengagement. With a quiet fading into the margins of their own lives. These are the men who stop texting back. Who stare blankly at screens. Who don't plan vacations, don't decorate rooms, don't respond to excitement or concern. They eat what's fast. Sleep when they can. Speak in short phrases. They're not in crisis, not visibly. But they're not here either. They've checked out, but left the lights on.

And this isn't laziness. It's neurological. Depression in men, especially when untreated, often shows up not as sadness but as emotional anesthesia. The term for it is anhedonia—the inability to feel pleasure or interest in things once enjoyed. It's common in trauma, burnout, chronic stress, and severe depression. And it devastates men differently than women. Because for many men, their sense of purpose is tethered to utility. To being effective. Useful. Capable. And when joy disappears, when meaning collapses, when they stop feeling anything—they lose that tether. They're not just sad. They're disoriented. Like they've lost gravity. And instead of falling apart, they fall inward. Quiet. Still. Gone.

Work is often the last thing to go. Many men maintain performance long after they've gone emotionally catatonic. They show up to meetings. They reply to emails. They handle tasks. But it's not pride that drives them—it's inertia. Motion without meaning. The job becomes the mask. The last acceptable form of participation. But when work dries up—or retirement comes, or layoffs hit, or burnout breaks through—the mask crumbles. And with it, the last thread of connection. This is why men who retire without a plan, without community, without an internal sense of self, often spiral into depression, substance abuse, or isolation. They weren't prepared for the silence. They were only trained to perform.

Romantic relationships don't fare much better. The disappearing man in a marriage or partnership isn't necessarily cruel. He's present. He does the dishes. He pays the bills. But he doesn't show up. He doesn't ask questions. Doesn't initiate affection. Doesn't talk about the future. Sex becomes mechanical or absent. Conversations become logistical. His partner feels it long before he does. Feels the absence, the drift, the ghost in the room wearing his clothes. And when they confront him, he says he's fine. Just tired. Just stressed. But he isn't tired. He's gone. And he doesn't know how to come back because he can't remember the last time he felt like a full person.

This erosion is especially common in men who've never had a language for emotion. Who were raised on toughness, taught that selfhood is optional and vulnerability is fatal. They never learned how to name what they felt, so when the internal world collapsed, they didn't scream. They just disappeared. Into routines. Into coping mechanisms. Into games and porn and passive scrolling. Into numbness. They didn't choose withdrawal. They fell into it. Slowly. And now it feels like the only state that's safe.

There's also a darker economic layer to all this. As industries shift and economies evolve, many men—especially those without higher education or flexible job skills—find themselves increasingly dislocated from opportunity. They see their identities tied to roles that no longer exist. Breadwinner. Builder. Provider. And when those identities evaporate, and no alternative is offered, they don't protest. They fade.

The percentage of men aged 25–54 not in the labor force has tripled in the last few decades. They are not all lazy. They are not all stoners. Many are hurting. Many are grieving the loss of purpose in a world that values productivity over personhood. And because no one's asking what they're feeling, they don't answer. They just stop trying.

And yet, we rarely talk about this form of male disappearance. Because it doesn't make headlines. It doesn't provoke outrage. It doesn't look violent. It looks like a man slowly turning to dust. And when people finally notice, they don't ask "What happened?" They ask "What's wrong with him?" As if this erosion was character, not consequence.

But it's not hopeless. Men can return. Can re-enter. Can reanimate. But they need a ladder. A path. And a reason. Not a rescue. Not a savior. A reason. Something that sparks meaning. A space that invites them back to themselves without judgment. Without pity. Without performance. They need to be seen before they can speak. Touched—emotionally, mentally, spiritually—before they can trust. And above all, they need permission. To be unfinished. To not have the answer. To want something more without knowing what it is.

This is where real healing begins. Not in asking a man to "open up," but in building a world where his silence isn't the only safe space he knows. Where disappearing is no longer the only response to pain. Where numbness isn't the price of being accepted. We need communities that notice when men fade—not just when they break. That ask questions before the retreat becomes permanent. That welcome the messy return, not just the triumphant comeback.

We also need to redefine male strength. Right now, many men think strength means endurance. And in some ways, it does. But not like this. Not the endurance of silence, of disconnection, of emotional vacancy. Strength should mean engagement. Presence. The willingness to feel, to care, to show up, even when it hurts. Especially when it hurts. And that requires a culture shift. One that doesn't just tell men "it's okay to talk," but also makes space for them to feel awkward, inarticulate, rusty, unsure—and loved anyway.

Because most men don't want to disappear. They just don't know another way to survive. The numbness wasn't a goal. It was a defense. And now it's a prison. But the door isn't locked. They just need someone to remind them how to walk out.

So if you're a man reading this and you've felt it—the slow fade, the vanishing act, the sense that you're watching your own life from somewhere far away—know this: You are not broken. You are not weak. You are not gone.

You are here.

You are tired.

You are still wanted.

And it's not too late to come back.

CHAPTER 10

Therapy Without the Fluff

If you've ever thought therapy was for broken people, weak people, people who cry a lot, or people who had childhoods so catastrophic they should come with a documentary voiceover—you're not alone. You're just misinformed. Because that's what most men have been sold: the idea that therapy is some fuzzy, self-indulgent process where you lie on a couch, blame your parents for everything, and pay someone to ask you how you feel for forty-five minutes while staring at a bookshelf full of scented candles. And if you're a man who prides himself on logic, on keeping your emotions buried six feet under, or on the myth that "pushing through" is always the answer, therapy probably seems about as useful as a gluten-free cookbook in a steakhouse. But that idea—the scoffing, the mockery, the skepticism—is killing us. Not just because therapy helps. But because it works best for the exact kind of man who's most likely to avoid it. This chapter is about what therapy actually is. What it isn't. Why most men misunderstand it. And how it can be one of the most practical, efficient, and even masculine tools for reclaiming control when life goes off the rails and staying sane when it hasn't yet—but you can feel the cracks coming.

Let's get this out of the way first: therapy is not magic. It's not a miracle. It doesn't "fix you." There's no dramatic breakthrough music. Most of the time it doesn't even feel like it's working—until suddenly, one day, you react differently than you used to. You don't snap at your partner. You don't binge-drink after a hard day. You don't spiral for a week because someone criticized you. You pause. You breathe. You recognize the pattern. You make a better move. That's therapy. That's the muscle memory of insight kicking in. And no, it doesn't happen overnight. But it's also not some endless emotional excavation project that forces you to relive your worst days forever. Done well, therapy is structured, strategic, and goal-oriented. And if you're a man who likes knowing how things work, therapy—real, grounded therapy—can give you a psychological blueprint for yourself. It's not about digging for trauma. It's about learning how to steer your own brain instead of being driven by it blindly through fire.

And yet, most men who need therapy the most avoid it like it's contagious. Why? Because it's unfamiliar. Because it requires vulnerability, and most men weren't trained to sit in that long enough to make it to insight. Because many therapists do use language that sounds soft, indirect, and annoying to someone used to blunt honesty. Because it's hard to know who to trust when your entire life has been spent faking composure. And because some men have tried therapy and it sucked. It felt irrelevant, vague, or worse—like emotional tourism. That's real. Not all therapy is good therapy. And not all therapists are good at speaking to men.

So let's talk about what actually works.

If you're a man who struggles with focus, overthinking, emotional flatness, anger, isolation, addictive behavior, perfectionism, panic, rage, or numbness—therapy can help. But you need the right kind. You don't need someone to hold your hand. You need someone who sees through your bullshit but doesn't shame you for it. Someone who gives you tools. Structure. Accountability. Someone who doesn't let you intellectualize your feelings until they disappear behind a smokescreen of cleverness. You need someone who can sit with silence without rushing to fill it. Someone who doesn't assume you're "resistant" when really you're just trying to figure out how to speak a language you were never taught.

Cognitive Behavioral Therapy (CBT) is a good start. It's focused, practical, and research-backed. It helps you identify the loops—those automatic, distorted thoughts that fuel anxiety, depression, shame, or rage—and gives you tangible ways to interrupt them. It's like debugging a system you didn't realize was running in the background. It's not about feelings instead of logic. It's about understanding that logic alone won't save you from a brain wired for pain avoidance. CBT helps you retrain that wiring. It works especially well for high-functioning men who feel stuck in old habits but don't understand why they can't break out.

Eye Movement Desensitization and Reprocessing (EMDR) is another evidence-based tool—especially for trauma. If you've got moments from the past that keep hitting you like sniper fire—flashbacks, panic attacks, guilt spirals, or unexplained reactions—EMDR can help process those frozen memories in a way that doesn't require endless retelling or years of talking. It works with how the brain stores trauma. Not in your words. In your wiring. And it doesn't require belief. It requires courage, consistency, and a willingness to trust the process more than the logic.

Group therapy—yes, even for men who hate groups—can be powerful too. But it has to be the right group. One that isn't drenched in toxic positivity or thinly veiled self-help marketing. Men's groups that are grounded, real, confidential, and moderated by skilled facilitators can create something most men haven't experienced since childhood: honest male connection without competition. Sitting in a room where another man says exactly what you've never dared to voice out loud—and doesn't get laughed at for it—can shift something deep. Can break the illusion that you're alone. That no one understands. That your shame is unique. Sometimes, the best therapy isn't what the therapist says—it's what another man dares to admit first.

But even one-on-one therapy, when done right, doesn't have to feel like exposure or punishment. A good therapist doesn't sit in judgment. They're not grading your masculinity. They're not there to tell you what you "should" do. They're a guide. A witness. A mirror. They don't fix you. They walk with you while you learn to do it yourself. And if that sounds weak, ask yourself this: What's more fragile—pretending you're okay while you crumble in silence, or stepping into a space where you finally get tools to stop faking it? You want strength? Sit in a room and tell the truth for the first time in your life. That's strength.

Still don't trust it? Fine. Start small. One session. No commitment. Tell the therapist straight up: "I'm skeptical. I don't trust this. I don't know what I'm doing here." The good ones will nod. They've heard it. They won't flinch. And if they do? Fire them. You're allowed to shop around. You're not married to the first therapist you try. This is your mind. Your time. Your money. Find someone who respects your pace, speaks your language, and challenges your bullshit without belittling your effort.

And no—you don't have to cry. You don't have to dig into your childhood if you're not ready. You don't have to journal, meditate, or talk about your dreams unless it actually helps. What you do have to do is show up. Consistently. Openly. Not perfectly. Just honestly. That's the hardest part for most men. Not the talking. The showing up. The not bailing after session three because it feels weird or you think you're wasting your time. Most breakthroughs don't feel like fireworks. They feel like boring, slow, almost imperceptible shifts. Like waking up one day and realizing you didn't hate yourself the way you used to. Like hearing your partner tell you something hard and not immediately shutting down. Like noticing your anger rise—and breathing instead of breaking something. That's therapy.

There are secular therapists who specialize in working with men. Use directories like Psychology Today, TherapyDen, Open Path, or Men's

Therapy Network. Look for terms like “trauma-informed,” “CBT,” “EMDR,” “men’s issues,” or “solution-focused.” And don’t be afraid to ask questions. Email them. Call them. Ask how they work. Ask if they’ve worked with men who were skeptical, angry, withdrawn, numb. If they hesitate? Move on. A therapist who doesn’t respect your starting point won’t help you get anywhere better.

For men in rural areas, financial hardship, or therapist deserts—online therapy platforms (like BetterHelp, Talkspace, or secular nonprofit organizations) can be better than nothing. Sliding scale options exist. Telehealth options exist. And no, it’s not as good as sitting in a room with someone—but it’s a start. And for some men, starting from the privacy of home is safer than sitting in a lobby wondering if someone you know will see you.

Above all, therapy only works when you stop trying to win it. It’s not a performance. You don’t get points for being self-aware. You don’t get medals for being stoic. It’s not a test. It’s a process. A recalibration. A slow stitching back together of the parts of you that got shredded by time, culture, pain, and silence. You don’t have to believe in it. You don’t have to feel ready. You just have to show up and tell the truth. And if you do it long enough, something will shift. You’ll remember your voice. You’ll stop running from your own reflection. You’ll start seeing the connections between your reactions and your past. Between your symptoms and your unspoken wounds. And then—if you’re lucky—you’ll stop feeling like a passenger in your own mind. You’ll start driving again.

Therapy is not a cure. But for many men, it’s the first place they learn how to live instead of just not dying. It’s not weakness. It’s self-respect. It’s accountability. It’s strategy. And most of all—it’s a return. To yourself. To your story. To the possibility that you’re not beyond repair. Just overdue for a tune-up.

So no fluff. No woo-woo. No incense. Just a chair, a professional, and your willingness to sit down and say, "Let's figure this out."

That's therapy. And it works.

CHAPTER 11

Brotherhood 2.0

Men need men. Not in some testosterone-fueled, alpha-male locker room way. Not in a "chug beer, bury feelings, and bond through violence" way. In the real way. The ancient way. The nervous-system-calming, shame-softening, soul-reminding way that men used to know before modern life drilled independence into them so hard they forgot the difference between autonomy and isolation. This chapter is about that difference—and about the crisis that's unfolded in its absence. It's about how brotherhood, in its truest form, isn't about toughness or tradition. It's about survival. And how rebuilding it—not as some nostalgic throwback, but as a conscious, evolved, and secular reinvention—isn't just helpful for men's mental health. It's essential.

Here's the uncomfortable truth: most adult men have no real friends. That's not an insult. It's a statistical reality. According to the Survey Center on American Life, in the last 30 years, the number of men who report having no close friends has quintupled. Half of men say they're unsatisfied with their friendships. One in five say they can't even name a single person they'd call in a crisis. And yet, if you ask them how they're doing, they'll say fine. Because they've been trained to see friendship not as a need, but as a luxury. Something optional. Something you grow out of. Something that happens naturally, or not at all. But friendship is not optional. Especially not for men. Especially not now. It's a structural necessity for mental resilience, for emotional regulation, for identity beyond work and romance. And without it, men fade. Quietly. Predictably. Tragically.

Part of the problem is that most men were never taught how to build friendships as adults. Male bonding in youth is usually based on shared activity, proximity, or competition—school, sports, games, work, joking. Emotional openness isn't part of the equation. Vulnerability is replaced by banter. Affection is buried under roasting. And while that surface-level bonding works in adolescence, it doesn't age well. Once life gets serious—marriage, kids, illness, loss, depression—those joke-based friendships don't hold up. Because you can't laugh your way through a breakdown. You can't fix grief with a meme. And if the only way you know how to connect with another man is by teasing him or talking about sports, then the moment life gets real, you're on your own. And most men are.

That loneliness becomes internalized. You start to think it's just you. That everyone else has this figured out. That you're the only one feeling left out, left behind, disconnected. So you stop reaching out. You stop initiating. You convince yourself it's better to just focus on work, or your partner, or your kids. And slowly, you disappear from your own social ecosystem. No one calls. No one checks in. Not because they don't care—but because they're just like you. Isolated. Busy. Tired. Ashamed. And when two isolated men each assume the other one doesn't care, nothing happens. No reconnection. No phone call. No second chance. Just silence. And silence, sustained long enough, becomes estrangement. And that estrangement becomes identity. You start to believe, This is just how it is now. But it doesn't have to be.

Rebuilding brotherhood doesn't mean recreating the past. It doesn't mean forming a band of brothers in the warrior-soldier-father mold of outdated masculinity. It means building spaces where men can show up without armor. Without performance. Without shame. It means cultivating friendships that aren't based on usefulness, status, or sarcasm—but on presence. And that starts with one very un-macho word: intentionality. Male friendships in adulthood don't happen by accident. They have to be made. Reached for. Protected. That means texting someone even when you're tired. Showing up to the thing you'd rather cancel. Asking better questions. Saying things like, "I miss hanging out. Let's get something on the calendar." It feels awkward at first. That's fine. It's a muscle. Use it.

But it's not just about trying harder. It's about building new models. We need spaces where male connection isn't secondary to something else. Not just bars. Not just gyms. Not just fantasy football. We need spaces where talking isn't weird. Where honesty isn't mocked. Where men can say, "I'm struggling," and not get met with a joke or a shrug. This is where peer groups come in. Men's groups. Support circles. Meetups. Online forums that aren't just rage pits or echo chambers. Think Men's Sheds in the UK—community-based workshops where men build things together and talk shoulder-to-shoulder, which studies have linked to reduced depression and increased life satisfaction. Think Evryman in the U.S.—facilitated emotional groups for men that focus on vulnerability, presence, and accountability. These aren't therapy groups. They're brotherhood labs. Places where men get to practice being fully human in front of other men—and learn that they won't be rejected for it.

And for the secular man, these spaces are even more critical. Because for centuries, religion provided this structure. The church group. The mosque gathering. The Shabbat table. Ritualized community, shared values, intergenerational wisdom. But as more men walk away from organized religion, they lose the scaffolding without replacing it. That's not a knock on deconstruction. It's a call to reconstruction. Brotherhood doesn't require faith. But it does require intention. Ritual. Practice. We need to normalize male friendships that are consistent, sacred, and chosen—not just convenient. We need secular circles where the structure of gathering isn't a sermon but a shared agreement: We show up for each other. Fully. Repeatedly. Without masks.

And no, this isn't always comfortable. Men raised in stoicism, sarcasm, or hyper-logic often find emotional connection with other men terrifying. It feels exposed. Cringey. Forced. But that's because it's unfamiliar—not because it's wrong. Neuroscience confirms what culture denies: men benefit massively from emotional attunement with other men. It regulates cortisol. It stabilizes the nervous system. It strengthens identity. You don't have to be touchy-feely to get this. You just have to be human. And whether it's a text chain with three good men who check in every week, or a monthly poker night where you go five percent deeper than the surface, the effect is the same: you remember you're not alone.

But to make brotherhood sustainable, we have to make it safe. That means holding each other accountable for presence without turning it into shame. It means saying, "Hey, you've been quiet lately. Are you okay?" and accepting "No, I'm not," without needing to fix it. It means listening. It means staying. It means learning the difference between banter and connection. Both have their place. But too many men hide behind humor and call it bonding. Real brotherhood goes deeper. Real brotherhood says, "I see you. I got you. Not just when you're fun. Not just when you're strong. Always."

This matters more than we can measure. Studies show that social isolation in men is directly linked to higher rates of substance abuse, suicide, cardiovascular disease, and early mortality. But when men have strong peer connections—real ones, not just fantasy league groups or job-based acquaintances—they live longer. Heal faster. Handle stress better. They parent better. Partner better. Think clearer. And maybe more importantly—they stop disappearing. Because they have people who would notice.

So how do you build this if you don't have it? Start small. One man. One message. One invite. One risk. Reach out to an old friend and say, "I know we haven't talked in a while, but I miss you." Start a monthly dinner. Join a men's group. Host one. Even just showing up consistently to a space—open mics, chess clubs, hikes—can become ritual. You don't need 50 men. You need three good ones. And one of them might be waiting for you to make the first move.

Also—drop the shame. It is not pathetic to want male friendship. It is not "gay" to say you love your friend. It is not needy to want deeper connection. That garbage narrative is what got us here. We don't need more tough guys with no tribe. We need men who know how to show up for each other even when it's awkward, even when it's hard, even when no one taught them how. Because that's how you break the cycle. Not alone. Together.

We call this chapter Brotherhood 2.0 because we're not asking men to regress. We're asking them to evolve. To build a new masculine culture rooted not in domination, detachment, or stoicism—but in courage, consistency, and emotional integrity. We're not trading strength for softness. We're expanding the definition of strength to include empathy. Vulnerability. Presence. And the kind of bond that doesn't just keep you from falling—but walks beside you when you already have.

Because no man was meant to go it alone. And the ones who say they are?

They're the ones who need it most.

CHAPTER 12

Rebuilding with Logic and Grace

When the floor drops out and there's no god to catch you, no divine purpose to explain your pain, no heaven waiting to reward your endurance—what's left? This is the brutal, unavoidable question modern men face when faith fails them, when inherited religion no longer fits the shape of their reality, when doctrine feels like a plastered smile over a hemorrhaging soul. Some leave church and don't miss a thing. Others leave and ache, not for God, but for the framework. For the ritual, the guidance, the shared vocabulary for pain. But in the secular void, we're not taught how to rebuild. We're just told to be free. To self-define. To Google a TED Talk and call it therapy. But freedom without form becomes chaos. And for men raised to suppress emotion, deconstructing belief without reconstructing meaning is a recipe for collapse. That's why this chapter exists—not to preach, not to convert, but to offer a roadmap for how to rebuild a life of purpose and resilience using the raw materials of secular wisdom. You don't need faith to feel. You need structure. You need something that doesn't ask you to kneel, but helps you stand.

Start with Stoicism. Not the Instagram quote version that turns Marcus Aurelius into a hustle bro, but the real thing. Stoicism isn't about being emotionless—it's about mastering the things you can control and releasing what you can't. For men drowning in anxiety, grief, and rage, this is oxygen. The world is a burning mess, yes. Your past is messy, your heart is heavy, your job sucks, your dad never said he was proud of you. That's real. But what matters, says Epictetus, is not what happens to you, but how you respond. What you choose. What you build from the wreckage. Stoicism is the art of not being ruled by pain, even when it's legitimate. And not because pain is weakness—but because your mind, your reason, your capacity for choice is stronger. If modern masculinity needs a new hero, let it be the man who can sit with grief without lashing out, who can walk through fire without pretending he doesn't feel the heat, who can say "this hurts" and "I will endure" in the same breath. That is not repression. That is refinement.

Then there's existentialism, the philosophical middle finger to cosmic meaninglessness. If Stoicism is about resilience, existentialism is about responsibility. Sartre, Camus, de Beauvoir—these were not optimists. They didn't offer hope as a guarantee. They stared into the abyss and said, "Fine. So there is no grand plan. Then I will make my own meaning." And for the modern man who feels invisible, optional, replaceable—this is power. You don't need a cosmic blueprint to justify your existence. You need to choose. Choose to show up. Choose to give a damn. Choose to be kind in a world that isn't. Choose to write your values in blood and sweat and action, even if no god is watching. Especially if no god is watching. Camus called this the "absurd hero"—the man who knows the universe is silent, and still gets out of bed to fight for beauty, justice, love, and truth, simply because he decides to. That's not bleak. That's defiant. That's grace, without asking for grace.

And humanism? That's where it all converges. Humanism says: we are enough. Not in a sappy, self-help way. In a grounded, gritty, historically-informed, fallible-but-still-worthy kind of way. It's the belief that we are capable of morality, dignity, compassion, and growth without divine mandate. That we can build better systems because we must, not because we fear hell. That science, empathy, and mutual care aren't just side notes—they're sacred in their own right. Humanism doesn't ignore suffering. It insists that we respond to it. That we ease it where we can. That we use our limited years not to escape pain but to lessen it—for ourselves and for others. And in a society that's told men for centuries that worth is earned through dominance or productivity, humanism reframes it entirely: your worth is not what you conquer or what you provide. It's your presence. Your impact. Your willingness to see others as fully human, and yourself as part of that same fragile, sacred whole.

Still, philosophy is not enough if it stays in the head. It has to move into the body, the calendar, the habits. Ritual doesn't belong to religion alone. You can build it yourself. A morning walk without headphones can be prayer. Journaling can be confession. Checking on your friend every Sunday can be liturgy. Sitting in silence, breathing through a panic attack, and not giving up—that's communion with the self. We rebuild our mental health not through grand epiphanies, but through small, repeated acts of self-loyalty. You don't need a church. You need a chair, a pen, a friend, a choice. You don't need a pastor. You need a practice.

Of course, none of this is easy. The religious world gives you scripts. Answers. Traditions. The secular path gives you questions. And if you're wired to fix things, to find certainty, to build with clear blueprints, this ambiguity feels threatening. But there's a quiet freedom here too. Because when you stop trying to be good for someone else's heaven, you start learning how to be whole in your own skin. You stop outsourcing morality. You start owning your impact. And when you fall—which you will—it's not sin. It's suffering. And suffering deserves care, not condemnation.

This approach also gives men a way to redefine failure. In faith-based models, failure often feels like moral collapse. A fall from grace. But in the secular philosophical space, failure is part of the process. The Stoic accepts setbacks. The existentialist expects despair. The humanist knows imperfection is the cost of agency. So instead of shaming yourself for not being okay, you start to track the patterns. You start to build strategies. Not to be perfect—but to keep going. Grace isn't granted from above. It's granted from within. And it comes in the form of accountability without cruelty. Effort without ego. Growth without performative virtue.

For the man who grew up with a Bible in one hand and a bottle of guilt in the other, this will take unlearning. It will feel foreign. Even wrong. Because you were trained to believe that moral strength only comes with divine permission. But look closer. Who holds you up in the storm? Your friend. Your therapist. Your own discipline. Your own choice to keep breathing when it's easier not to. That is sacred. That is strength. And the secular world, when embraced with clarity and courage, gives you space to hold it.

And yes, you will still long for transcendence. That's human. But transcendence doesn't require myth. It can come in the form of awe at a sunrise, or tears during a song, or the electric stillness of holding your child's hand. You don't need heaven to feel wonder. You just need to notice. To stay open. To stop numbing. To let beauty in even when it doesn't fix anything. That's the quiet art of being alive in a brutal world. That's secular grace.

Rebuilding your inner life without religion also gives you a strange new gift: the ability to see others clearly. When you no longer believe suffering is punishment, or that joy is reward, you start to treat people more gently. More curiously. You stop trying to fit them into moral hierarchies. You stop needing to rank yourself. You just become a man among men. Flawed. Growing. Capable of harm, yes—but also capable of healing. And that means the work you do to tend to your own mind, your own heart, your own trauma—it ripples. It models something. It gives other men permission. Not because you're preaching. But because you exist as proof that there is another way.

So where do you start? Read the Stoics, yes. Read Camus. Read bell hooks. Read Baldwin. Read Nietzsche, if you're brave and slightly masochistic. But more than that—apply. Take one concept and wear it for a week. "I will not react to what I cannot control." "I will act as if my choices matter." "I will hold space for pain without labeling it weakness." Let philosophy become muscle. Let values become verbs. Let your secular belief system be a thing you live, not just a thing you quote.

And above all—let grace be your own. You do not need forgiveness from a sky god to move forward. You need to forgive yourself for being human in a world that breaks humans. You need to forgive your father for not having the tools. You need to forgive the younger version of you who coped however he could. And you need to offer that same forgiveness to others—not because they deserve it, but because carrying poison is not a sign of strength. Putting it down is. That is what rebuilding looks like. Not grand declarations. Just a man who refuses to stay broken, who pieces himself back together using the bricks others left behind, and who walks forward—not toward perfection, but toward peace.

You don't need faith to feel.

You need permission.

And you can give that to yourself.

Right now.

Today.

CHAPTER 13

Raising Better Sons

We can't change the fathers we had, but we sure as hell can change the sons we raise. And if there's any hope of breaking this brutal cycle—of silenced grief, duct-taped rage, and numbed-out men sleepwalking through their lives—it starts here. Not in policy papers or think tanks or inspirational memes. It starts in bedrooms and living rooms, in whispered apologies and awkward questions, in the space between a father's restraint and a son's uncertainty. For too long, boys have been handed a blueprint that teaches toughness over tenderness, control over curiosity, and success over self-awareness. And the result isn't just trauma—it's confusion. It's sons who grow into men unsure of how to feel without shame, how to love without armor, how to ask for help without fear of being seen as weak. They inherit silence like a birthright. And if we want to interrupt that inheritance, we have to get loud about what better looks like. We have to raise boys who don't have to bleed just to prove they're alive. Who don't have to bury themselves just to be accepted. Who don't have to spend thirty years unlearning what they were never meant to carry in the first place.

Raising better sons isn't about raising softer boys. It's about raising emotionally literate humans. It's about building the kind of internal scaffolding that allows a boy to cry without crumbling, to get angry without causing harm, to feel scared and not shrink from himself. And it starts early. Before they know the words for depression or anxiety or shame, boys already absorb the cues we send them—when we flinch at their tears, when we interrupt their sadness with distraction, when we reward stoicism and ridicule sensitivity. The damage isn't always loud.

Sometimes it's a father who stiffens instead of hugging. A teacher who calls a quiet boy "timid" but praises the loud one for "leadership." A coach who tells a kid to "man up" after a bad hit. It's a thousand tiny cuts that tell a boy: your feelings are dangerous, and your worth is tied to how well you suppress them. And even in homes full of love, this programming seeps in, because it's cultural. It's ancestral. It's been baked into the soil of masculinity for centuries. That doesn't mean we're doomed. It means we have to be intentional.

Intentional parenting—whether you're a biological parent, a step-parent, a mentor, or just a man who interacts with boys—means modeling what emotional health looks like in real time. It means naming your own feelings instead of bottling them. It means apologizing when you screw up instead of posturing. It means letting your son see you struggle with something and work through it—not perfectly, but humanly. Because boys don't learn how to be men from lectures. They learn by watching. And if what they see is a man who never expresses vulnerability, who drowns his exhaustion in whiskey or rage or silence, who only ever shows strength in its most brittle form—then that's what they'll become, too. You can talk about empathy all you want. But if they never see it, they'll never learn it. And they'll grow up thinking emotional honesty is a liability, not a skill.

We also have to rethink the way we discipline. Not to let boys run wild, but to move away from fear-based obedience toward responsibility-based growth. The old-school model of discipline—punishment without explanation, shame without context—might get short-term compliance, but it doesn't teach accountability. It teaches fear. And boys who learn to associate mistakes with humiliation will grow into men who either hide their failures or double down to avoid admitting them. What they need instead is consequence paired with reflection. Not just "You did wrong," but "Let's talk about why that happened and how you can do better next time." That sounds soft. It's not. It's harder than yelling. It takes more patience, more presence, more clarity. But it plants something deeper. It teaches that being wrong doesn't mean being worthless. That messing up doesn't mean being unloved. That accountability and shame are not the same thing.

Language matters, too. We have to stop talking about boys like they're ticking time bombs or future predators-in-training. We have to stop describing healthy emotion as feminine and start describing it as human. Stop saying "man up" and start saying "feel it, face it, fix it." Stop mocking boys for being dramatic and start asking what's underneath it. Stop assuming that silence means they're okay. Because often, the quietest boys are the ones holding the heaviest things. And if they grow up hearing nothing but jokes about how "boys will be boys" or how "real men don't cry," they will internalize a version of manhood so small it will crush them from the inside out. Then they'll either implode, explode, or disappear. And we'll wonder why.

Of course, this all becomes even harder in a culture that constantly undermines these efforts. Boys are still bombarded with media that tells them their worth lies in dominance, in detachment, in sexual conquest, in physical strength, in never needing anyone. And if they don't fit that mold—if they're soft-spoken or artistic or anxious or questioning—they're seen as defective. Or worse, as failures. That's where we, the adults in their lives, have to become a counter-narrative. We have to say, out loud and often: there are a million ways to be a man. And all of them are valid if they're rooted in integrity, empathy, and growth. We have to give them better stories. Books, films, music, conversations. Let them see men who cry, men who nurture, men who question, men who grow. Show them that masculinity isn't a straitjacket. It's a spectrum. A toolkit. And they get to decide which tools to use—not because they're trying to prove something, but because they're building a life that feels whole.

This gets especially complex when we talk about single-parent households, or homes where fathers are absent. The data is clear: boys who grow up without stable male role models are at increased risk for depression, aggression, poor academic performance, and criminal involvement. But that doesn't mean the absence of a father dooms a boy. It just means we need to widen the net. Coaches. Uncles. Mentors. Community leaders. Teachers. We need a culture where men see themselves as collectively responsible for the emotional health of the next generation—not in a condescending, hero-complex way, but in a consistent, present, I-got-you kind of way. And for those men who were abandoned, who don't know how to father because they never had one—there's grace here, too. You can learn. You can change the narrative. You can become the man you needed. You don't have to be perfect. You just have to show up and keep trying.

Co-parenting is also critical in this equation. Mothers, nonbinary parents, and caregivers of all kinds need to be partners in this work, not just emotional support units or default disciplinarians. Raising emotionally healthy boys is a team effort. It requires alignment. It requires shared language. It requires breaking out of the gendered scripts where mom is the "feelings parent" and dad is the "tough parent." That division is not just outdated—it's dangerous. Because it teaches boys that empathy is something mom handles, and authority is something dad enforces. That kindness is maternal, and strength is paternal. When in fact, both are human. And when a boy sees both parents modeling emotional fluency, conflict resolution, mutual respect, and accountability, he doesn't have to choose between love and leadership. He learns they're intertwined.

And yes—this is exhausting. Because while we're trying to raise better sons, we're still healing the broken boys inside ourselves. We're still navigating our own trauma, our own blind spots, our own programming. We're still trying to pay bills and show up and not lose our minds. But here's the truth: your healing is their inheritance. Every time you choose to listen instead of lash out, to admit fear instead of deny it, to show up when you'd rather shut down—you're teaching your son that being a man doesn't mean being unbreakable. It means being real. Being present. Being accountable. Being alive. And that lesson, more than any lecture or rule or punishment, will echo through his life long after you're gone.

Raising better sons is how we change the world. Not through slogans or sermons, but through consistent, messy, vulnerable, grounded presence. Through choosing connection over control. Curiosity over condemnation. Love over legacy. Let the boy cry, so the man doesn't have to bleed. That's not weakness. That's evolution.

CHAPTER 14

Men at the Margins

For all the ink spilled, all the workshops booked, and all the awareness campaigns slapped on hashtags and billboards, there's one truth that continues to get swept under the rug when we talk about men's mental health: not all men start from the same place. The crisis is not monolithic, and neither are its casualties. When we talk about suicide rates, substance abuse, incarceration, or depression, we're often talking about numbers in aggregate—averages, trends, clusters. But beneath those averages are lives that don't fit neatly into the margins of PowerPoint slides. Black men, gay men, trans men, poor men, disabled men, immigrant men—men who live outside the mythological "default male" template of straight, white, cisgender, able-bodied, middle-class normalcy—are disproportionately left to fend for themselves in a system that was never built for them in the first place. The conversations, the support groups, the therapy models, the Instagram slogans—they often speak in generic tones designed to soothe the comfortably struggling. But if you're a man at the margins, struggling doesn't feel comfortable. It feels like drowning in silence while being told the life raft is "coming soon"—but only if you speak the right way, look the right way, and survive long enough to be seen.

Let's start with race. The Black male experience of mental health is a minefield of double-edged expectations. On one side, there's the legacy of systemic racism: poverty, over-policing, incarceration, generational trauma, and a culture that pathologizes Black emotion as threat. On the other, there's the cultural expectation of strength, of stoicism, of "being twice as good to get half as far." Mental health struggles in Black communities—especially among men—are often met with silence, shame, or spiritual outsourcing. "Pray on it." "Man up." "Don't air our business." These are not malicious responses; they are protective mechanisms in communities that have been systemically stripped of trust in healthcare systems, therapists, and institutional safety nets. And for good reason. Studies have shown that Black men are more likely to be misdiagnosed with schizophrenia instead of mood disorders, more likely to be criminalized for emotional outbursts, less likely to be offered therapeutic options instead of medication or confinement. So when a Black man struggles with depression, he's not just facing the illness—he's facing a system wired to interpret his pain as danger.

Now factor in economic class. Poverty doesn't just make life harder; it makes suffering invisible. Working-class and poor men—regardless of race—often have limited access to healthcare, live in mental health deserts, and are more likely to be overworked, underinsured, and trapped in environments where therapy sounds like a luxury for people who can afford "self-discovery." When rent is due, kids are hungry, and the car's three months behind on payments, there's no time to process feelings. Survival becomes the full-time job. And let's be honest: the aesthetics of modern therapy—clean couches, soft lighting, Instagram therapists in cozy cardigans—often alienate men who grew up hard. If you're a construction worker, an ex-con, or a dishwasher pulling double shifts, you don't want to be patronized or "guided through your inner child." You want real talk, real tools, and real respect. But that's rarely what you get when the entire system has been built to soothe fragile egos, not fortify fractured spirits.

Let's not forget LGBTQ+ men. Gay, bi, trans, and queer men live with layers of trauma that stack like a psychological Jenga tower. From childhood bullying and religious condemnation to societal erasure and targeted violence, they carry wounds that often fester in silence. Even in "progressive" spaces, mental health support can be riddled with subtle bias—therapists assuming gender roles, dismissing sexuality as incidental, or downplaying the long-term impact of identity-based trauma. Trans men face an especially brutal gauntlet: gender dysphoria, social exclusion, medical discrimination, and the constant existential weight of being politicized simply for existing. And if they reach out for help? They're often misgendered, questioned, or met with clueless platitudes. The data doesn't lie: LGBTQ+ men are significantly more likely to suffer from depression, anxiety, suicidal ideation, and substance abuse. Yet they're less likely to receive effective, affirming care. Why? Because even the world of mental health is steeped in heteronormative assumptions and outdated binaries. When we say "men," most institutions hear "straight, cis, emotionally constipated." And the rest are left to figure it out alone.

And then there are disabled men—those living with physical, cognitive, or neurological impairments. Here the marginalization is twofold: society often treats disabled people as either inspirational props or burdens to be pitied, and mental health discourse often overlooks them entirely. For disabled men, masculinity is complicated by societal narratives that equate manhood with physical capability, sexual performance, and independence. When your body doesn't "cooperate," the world starts to question your manhood by default. And mental health support? Often inaccessible, unaffordable, or simply ill-suited to the realities of disabled life. Try finding a therapist who understands both PTSD and chronic pain, or who can hold space for a man navigating both internal shame and external inaccessibility. It's rare. And that rarity means many disabled men suffer in silence, forced to wear a mask of "resilience" while their pain is either fetishized or ignored.

Immigrant men, too, sit on the edge of cultural translation and psychological overload. Whether fleeing war, poverty, persecution, or just chasing the myth of a better life, many carry trauma they cannot name in a language they do not speak. Add to that the pressures of assimilation, financial instability, legal insecurity, and cultural dislocation—and you have a mental health cocktail spiked with isolation, shame, and a deeply ingrained survival reflex. Therapy often assumes a baseline of cultural context that immigrants don't share. Expressions of emotion, family dynamics, religious values, and even body language can be misread by well-meaning but untrained professionals. For many immigrant men, help exists—but it doesn't feel like it's for them. And when you've crossed oceans just to survive, the idea of paying someone to unpack your trauma can feel both absurd and indulgent.

Even the language we use when we talk about "men's mental health" is often coded. We say things like "let's redefine masculinity," but we rarely say whose masculinity we're redefining. Is it the stoic Wall Street executive? The suburban dad with repressed grief? What about the young Black man hustling side gigs to keep the lights on? The trans man navigating hormone therapy and street harassment? The disabled vet who can't find work and won't go back to the VA because last time they gave him pills and a pamphlet and called it care? The term "men" should be a banner wide enough to cover every man. But too often, it functions like a velvet rope—letting some in while leaving others outside to rot.

Intersectionality isn't just academic jargon. It's the damn blueprint for reality. And if your solution doesn't account for how race, gender identity, class, sexuality, and ability intersect with masculinity, then your solution is incomplete at best—and harmful at worst. One-size-fits-all doesn't fit anyone. It just fits the people who were always centered to begin with.

So what do better solutions look like? They look like culturally competent therapy that doesn't tokenize or exoticize but meets men where they are. They look like peer-led groups tailored to specific communities—Black men supporting Black men, queer men gathering in safety, immigrant men unpacking trauma in their mother tongue. They look like mental health education embedded in barbershops, gyms, mosques, shelters, and schools. They look like therapists who listen more than they interpret, who ask before assuming, who do the work of understanding lived experiences that differ from their own. They look like funding community initiatives instead of just launching awareness campaigns. They look like training clinicians in racial bias, trans competency, disability advocacy, and trauma-informed care. They look like justice.

And to be clear, this isn't about coddling anyone. It's about precision. You don't treat a heart condition with ibuprofen, and you don't treat marginalized mental health struggles with generic advice. You need the right tools for the right wounds. And that means investing in the hard work of listening, adapting, and rebuilding systems that have failed too many for too long.

None of this will be easy. Systemic change never is. But the alternative is the status quo—and the status quo is killing people. Men at the margins are not just statistics. They are brothers, sons, fathers, lovers, neighbors, leaders. They are full human beings with stories that deserve to be heard and healed—not shoehorned into a framework built for someone else's comfort.

The future of men's mental health won't be found in mass-market platitudes or one-size-fits-all therapy. It'll be found at the edges, in the messy, beautiful complexity of real lives lived far from the spotlight. It'll be found in specificity, in humility, in the unglamorous work of equity.

And if we don't do that work—if we keep pretending the margins are optional—we'll keep losing people we never really saw.

CHAPTER 15

Unlearning the Old World

Let's be blunt: the world we inherited was not designed with emotional survival in mind. It was built by men who feared vulnerability, enforced dominance, and outsourced care. It was reinforced by systems that rewarded emotional suppression, punished deviation, and laughed off introspection as weakness. That world—this old world—was never sustainable. It produced conquest and cruelty in equal measure, praised hollow strength while burying real pain, and left generations of men emotionally amputated, functionally numb, and too ashamed to ask why. And now that it's unraveling, now that cracks are showing in the stoic armor and the suicide graphs climb like silent obituaries, we are left with a brutal question: how do we unlearn the old world before it kills more of us? How do we deconstruct manhood without erasing it? How do we build new models of mental wellness that include men not as ticking time bombs or tragic statistics but as human beings with minds worth mending, hearts worth hearing, and identities worth evolving? This chapter is not about nuance. It's about demolition, reconstruction, and choosing courage over comfort. The old world must die so that real healing can begin.

Start with the workplace—the petri dish where outdated masculinity metastasizes into performance-driven toxicity. For generations, men were told that their value hinged on output. You are what you produce. You are your title, your wage, your willingness to sacrifice your body and mind on the altar of industry. Exhaustion was a badge of honor. Mental health was a personal failing. Burnout was rebranded as "commitment." Now, we know better. The data screams it: men in high-demand jobs suffer elevated rates of heart disease, depression, substance abuse, and suicide. Yet even in 2025, most workplaces are woefully behind when it comes to mental health support tailored for men. Corporate wellness programs often amount to yoga mats and meditation apps—tools that may soothe but rarely address the root issue: a culture that incentivizes suppression, penalizes honesty, and pathologizes emotion unless it's anger. What's needed isn't a mandatory mindfulness seminar. What's needed is policy. Real, enforceable policy. Paid mental health leave that doesn't require emotional striptease. Access to therapy covered under insurance without labyrinthine codes and stigma. Flexible scheduling for therapy appointments, parenting duties, or just human recovery. Training for managers not to gaslight or micromanage but to recognize distress and respond with humanity. And perhaps most importantly, an internal cultural shift that recognizes vulnerability as strength—not PR-speak, but policy-backed praxis. A workplace where a man can say "I'm not okay" without risking his job or his dignity isn't just humane—it's efficient. Because a burnt-out man is a liability. A supported one is a powerhouse.

But the workplace is only one front. The media—our mirror and our molder—is another battlefield where outdated ideas of masculinity keep getting reheated and served with a side of irony. The modern man, if you believe our screens, is either the emotionally unavailable alpha, the bumbling man-child, or the broken anti-hero who drinks too much, kills without remorse, and heals by exacting revenge. Occasionally, we get a "sensitive" guy—usually played for laughs or written by someone who thinks crying once a decade makes a man evolved. These stereotypes aren't just lazy. They're lethal. They reinforce the idea that male pain is only valid if it's violent, that male growth must be tragic, and that emotional literacy is optional rather than essential. We need better stories. Period. We need novels, shows, games, and films that show men navigating depression without a body count, processing grief without a gun, confronting trauma without turning into a savior or a sociopath. We need stories where men raise children with tenderness, express fear without shame, and find purpose not in domination but in connection. Representation matters not just for those watching—but for those living. When young boys see nothing but stoic warriors or comic relief on screen, they learn to armor up or clown down. Neither leaves space for authenticity. And the consequences spill into every part of their lives: their friendships, their partnerships, their silence. The media doesn't need to "cancel" masculinity. It needs to rewrite it with nuance, respect, and a recognition that real men cry, break, rebuild, and sometimes—miraculously—get better.

Now let's talk education, because if we don't catch this early, we're just putting out fires while the house keeps burning. Most boys are emotionally fluent until society beats it out of them. Watch a four-year-old boy cry when his friend leaves the playground. Watch a seven-year-old talk about missing his mom. The rawness is there—until it's shamed, mocked, or punished. By age ten, many boys have already learned to self-censor, to swap softness for sarcasm, vulnerability for violence, or connection for conquest. Schools reinforce this through gendered discipline, heteronormative health curriculums, and a general failure to teach emotional literacy as a core subject. What if we changed that? What if emotional intelligence was taught with the same rigor as math? What if boys were taught to name their feelings, to regulate their responses, to see empathy not as feminine but as fundamental to human survival? What if school counselors were trained in male psychology beyond generic stress management? What if we created rites of passage that weren't about harm or hazing but about integrity, emotional honesty, and contribution to community? The old world told boys to harden. The new one must teach them to listen—first to themselves, then to others. If we embed emotional fluency early, we don't just reduce future crises. We raise men who can weather storms without becoming one.

And what of the systems—the policies and institutions that still treat male mental health like a punchline or an afterthought? The justice system still disproportionately criminalizes symptoms of mental illness in men. Homelessness interventions rarely address male trauma. Veteran care is still drowning in bureaucracy. Substance abuse programs often ignore the emotional roots of dependency in favor of punitive abstinence models. Even mental health campaigns, despite their growing presence, often miss the mark—offering vague "talk to someone" slogans without acknowledging that most men don't know where to start, who to trust, or how to explain what they're feeling in language that won't get them dismissed. Reform must be comprehensive. It must involve re-educating healthcare professionals on male-specific symptom profiles—because men's depression often looks like rage, detachment, or workaholism. It must include policy-level investment in peer-led support models, especially for marginalized men. It must involve integrating mental health checks into primary care. It must involve stopping the mockery—yes, the mockery—of men who dare to speak. Late night shows, sitcoms, and online comments still default to sarcasm and emasculation when a man says he's in therapy, cries publicly, or admits to mental strain. We must create a society where a man's breakdown isn't a meme but a signal. Not a red flag, but a red light—telling us to slow down, pay attention, and offer something better than a punchline.

All of this boils down to a single, radical truth: masculinity is not broken. But the way we've been told to perform it is. The old model—dominance, silence, self-sacrifice, emotional constipation—is obsolete. It served empire-building, not humanity. It protected systems, not souls. If we want a future where men don't just survive but thrive, we need to redefine manhood not as a retreat from emotion, but as a reckoning with it. A man is not weak for asking for help. He's not feminine for crying. He's not soft for admitting fear. He's whole. He's present. He's powerful in the only way that actually matters: through authenticity. And that redefinition must come not just from psychologists and activists—but from everyday men. From barbershops and boardrooms. From locker rooms and lunch breaks. From artists and athletes and fathers and sons. The next generation will model what we embody. If we want different outcomes, we have to offer different examples.

That means you. Yes, you. If you're reading this, you are part of the unlearning. Whether you're a therapist, a teacher, a father, a friend, a man yourself, or someone who loves one—your voice matters. Your vulnerability matters. Your willingness to call out the mockery, to challenge the lazy jokes, to create space for real talk—it all matters. The revolution won't be televised. It will be whispered across lunch tables, spoken in therapy rooms, carved into art, shouted in protest, lived out in small choices that add up to something seismic. We will not heal the wounds of masculinity by pretending they don't exist. We will not stop the silent suicides by offering slogans. We will not end the loneliness epidemic by waiting for someone else to fix it.

The old world was loud, rigid, cruel, and afraid of softness. Let the new world be brave, curious, compassionate, and unashamed of the full human experience. Let it be a place where a man can feel without fear, heal without ridicule, and speak without needing to preface his pain. Let it be a place where no boy learns that love must be earned, that strength means silence, or that his worth depends on how much he can carry without crying.

Unlearning the old world will take time. It will take failure. It will take us holding each other accountable with kindness instead of contempt. But it is possible. We know this because the current generation of men is already asking the questions their fathers buried. They are sitting in circles instead of corners. They are redefining success to include peace. They are telling their sons "it's okay to cry"—and meaning it. They are becoming, slowly and imperfectly, the kind of men the world has always needed: whole, honest, and here.

CONCLUSION

Saying It Out Loud

This is the part where the silence ends. Where we stop whispering into voids and start shouting into spaces that never bothered to make room for us. This is the part where statistics step aside and stories take the microphone. Where we dare to say what we should've said years ago—that we're not okay, that we've been drowning in plain sight, and that the culture that raised us to be tough, silent, useful, and emotionally bulletproof has left us brittle, haunted, and half-alive. This is the part where we stop blaming biology, shrugging off despair as fate, or waiting for someone else to speak first. Because the crisis we're in—the slow bleed of broken men—is not about silence by nature. It's about silence by design. A design built by fear, reinforced by shame, and passed down like a disease we never asked for. But what's been passed down can be put down. And what we refuse to name cannot heal. So we say it now. Loud. Clear. Together. The pain is real. The wounds are deep. But the silence stops here.

If you've made it this far—through the numbers, the narratives, the science, the systems, and the stories—then you already know the truth: this is not a fringe issue. This is not a soft concern tucked behind more "serious" topics. Men's mental health is not a charity case or a political pawn. It is the quiet fulcrum on which families, communities, economies, and futures are precariously balanced. When men fall apart, it rarely looks like tears—it looks like violence, addiction, collapse, and ghosting. It looks like the father who vanishes, the friend who OD's, the colleague who explodes, the son who disappears into his own silence. And yet, even now, society meets this implosion with memes, mockery, or metaphors—never the full gravity it deserves. Even now, we tell men to "get help" without building them any bridges toward it. We cheer mental health awareness while shaming emotional expression. We want men to be better partners, better fathers, better humans—without ever asking what it would take for them to feel safe enough to be fully human themselves. That hypocrisy is killing people. And the only cure is honesty. Brutal, blinding, truth-soaked honesty that tears through the bullshit like sunlight through fog. That honesty starts with saying it out loud.

Say what? Say the hard things. Say the things you were told made you weak. Say, "I'm not sure who I am anymore." Say, "I feel like I'm failing and I don't know how to stop." Say, "I'm angry all the time and I don't know why." Say, "I need help, but I'm scared to ask." Say, "This pressure is suffocating me." Say, "I've been pretending for so long that I forgot how to feel." Say, "I don't want to die, but I'm not really living either." Say, "I don't want to be the strong one today." Say, "I'm tired of surviving instead of existing." And say it not as a confession of weakness but as a declaration of truth. Because truth, when said aloud, doesn't just set you free—it gives someone else the permission they didn't know they needed to stop pretending too. It shatters the illusion of aloneness. And in a world where loneliness is now a public health crisis, where male isolation is both epidemic and invisible, a single honest sentence can be a lifeline. Say it for yourself. Say it for your brother. Say it for your father who never could. Say it for the boy you used to be—the one who still lives in the corner of your ribcage, wondering why he was told not to cry.

But don't stop there. Honesty is only the ignition. Action is the fuel. So we move—imperfectly, courageously, and collectively. We challenge our workplaces to stop measuring value in output and start investing in human wholeness. We create policies that make mental health access real, not rhetorical. We build schools that teach boys how to name what they feel before they bury it. We tell stories that make room for male grief, joy, fear, and softness without apology. We raise sons who don't inherit our silence and daughters who expect more from the men in their lives than emotional vacancy. We design public health campaigns that speak the language of real men—not the sanitized slogans of PR firms. We normalize therapy without caveats. We build communities that are secular, honest, and built on shared vulnerability—not performance or punishment. We model what it means to fall apart without shame and rebuild without bravado. And we never again allow mockery, dismissal, or deflection to be the final word when a man breaks his silence.

We also hold space—for the men who never made it. For the ones who didn't speak. For the ones who were too far gone. For the ones whose pain outpaced their hope. We say their names, even if just in our hearts. We do not romanticize their suffering, but we refuse to erase them. Every man who dies by suicide, every man swallowed by addiction or isolation, every man who vanishes behind the walls of shame—we carry their memory into the work we now do. They are the caution. They are the reason. They are the fire in our chest that reminds us why silence is no longer an option. We honor them not with platitudes but with prevention. Not with guilt, but with grit.

This book made a choice not to lean on faith. Not because faith has no value, but because too many men have been told that belief is their only path to meaning. That without religion, they are unanchored, unredeemable, unworthy of comfort or healing. That lie has cost lives. Because when non-religious men suffer, society often has no language for their pain. No sanctuary that isn't sanctified. No rituals that don't require worship. But the truth is this: meaning is not exclusive to religion. Healing is not reserved for the faithful. You do not need to believe in a god to believe in your own worth. You do not need to worship to be whole. You do not need a savior to deserve saving. What you need is truth. What you need is people. What you need is language that honors your reality, scaffolding that holds space for your grief, and community that doesn't require conversion—just presence. That's what this book aimed to give. A godless gospel of grit, grace, and getting through it. Not perfectly. Not peacefully. But powerfully.

So here's where we land: if you're a man reading this, know this book was written for you not as a diagnosis, but as a mirror. Not to fix you, but to tell you that you are not broken in the way you think. You are hurting. You are human. And you are not alone. If you feel lost, that is not failure. It's evidence that the old map no longer works. Burn it. Draw a new one. One that includes therapy, friendship, emotion, rest, and purpose that isn't defined by how much you can endure before collapsing. If you feel ashamed, know this: shame is a parasite. It thrives in silence. Starve it with honesty. If you don't know where to start, start here—with one sentence. One text. One question. One truth. If you love a man, this book was also for you. To understand him better. To stop expecting emotional translation. To meet him where he is, not where the world says he should be. To listen without fixing. To witness without judgement. To remind him that he matters—not because of what he does, but because of who he is when the masks come off.

If you work with men—as a therapist, a teacher, a policy-maker, a coach, a healthcare worker—this book was for you too. A call to do better. To stop assuming. To learn how male depression speaks in code. To stop treating masculinity like a diagnosis and start treating it like a context. To meet men with language they understand, environments they trust, and interventions that honor their lived experience. The next evolution in mental health care won't be a new app or a miracle pill. It'll be an honesty revolution. A dismantling of stigma that starts with those brave enough to speak.

So we say it now, one last time. The silence ends here. The crisis is not just personal—it's collective. But so is the healing. This book is not the solution. It's a spark. What you do next is the flame. Talk. Listen. Build. Show up. Break the cycle. Ask your friends real questions. Answer them with something other than "I'm good." Leave room for the long pauses. The tears. The awkward honesty. The messy beginnings. And when someone finally says it out loud, when someone breaks and lets it spill—don't flinch. Don't fix. Just stay. Just witness. Just be the kind of person this world never taught us how to be: present, patient, and painfully human.

Because that's how we save lives. Not with perfection. Not with promises. But with presence. With saying it out loud. And not backing down.

APPENDIX

Resources, Sources, and the Road Ahead

Let's make this as real and useful as possible. Because the crisis we've spent this entire book unraveling isn't theoretical. It's not academic, abstract, or fodder for social media discourse. It's lived. It's relentless. And it's right now. So this appendix is not an afterthought—it's a toolkit. A map for the men who don't know where to turn, the allies who want to help, the professionals ready to listen, and the skeptics on the verge of believing that change, somehow, might still be possible. The pages before this one were built to reveal. What comes next is built to restore. You don't need a miracle or a mantra. You need real resources, data you can trust, and stories that remind you this pain is survivable—and that healing isn't only for the religious, the poetic, or the already halfway okay. It's for you. Right now. No matter how hollow, angry, numb, or lost you feel.

So we begin with the essentials—because sometimes surviving the night is more urgent than philosophizing about the month. If you or someone you care about is in crisis, forget the stigma, the bravado, or the shame-drenched narratives. Go straight for help. In the U.S., dial or text 988 to reach the Suicide & Crisis Lifeline. It's fast, free, and judgment-free. For veterans, press 1 after dialing 988 to be routed to a VA responder. If you need immediate medical attention, call 911—yes, even if your brain tells you not to be dramatic. You are not dramatic. You're a human being who matters. If you're outside the U.S., here are a few key global lifelines: Samaritans UK at 116 123, Lifeline Australia at 13 11 14, and Crisis Services Canada at 1-833-456-4566. If you hate phones (as many do), go digital: Crisis Text Line offers 24/7 support in the U.S., Canada, and the UK—just text HELLO to 741741. Prefer anonymity? Online platforms like 7 Cups, BlahTherapy, or Reddit's r/Men'sLib provide low-pressure spaces to unload, ask questions, and realize you're not the only one falling apart.

Now, for those ready to take the next step: therapy. Not the unicorn-riding kind that insists on deep breathing while you're still trying not to punch drywall—but real, grounded, evidence-based therapy. Not all therapists are created equal, and not all are a good fit for secular men. You want someone who understands your context—your skepticism, your frustration, your aversion to emotional clichés. Start at PsychologyToday.com—yes, it's clunky, but it has a massive, filterable database. Select "Men's Issues" under specialties, and look for someone trained in CBT (Cognitive Behavioral Therapy), EMDR (for trauma), ACT (Acceptance and Commitment Therapy), or IFS (Internal Family Systems) if you're dealing with chronic guilt, shame, or identity confusion. Sites like TherapyDen, Open Path Collective (low-cost therapy), and Inclusive Therapists (if race, gender, or LGBTQIA+ sensitivity is important) also offer great directories. For secular-specific mental health, check out the Secular Therapy Project—they specialize in connecting non-religious clients with non-religious clinicians, removing the awkward dance of tiptoeing around prayer, dogma, or cosmic platitudes when all you really need is a damn lifeline.

Can't afford therapy? That doesn't mean you're out of options. Try online peer support groups designed specifically for men. Evryman, MensGroup.com, and Men's Sheds (especially popular in Australia and the UK) provide non-clinical spaces to connect with other guys who are also tired of pretending. These aren't macho jerk-fests or pickup artist echo chambers. They're real-talk communities where it's okay to say, "I don't know how to do this," and be met with nods instead of judgment. If you prefer digital connection, forums like r/MensLib, r/DecidingToBeBetter, and NoStupidQuestions on Reddit can be weirdly therapeutic when you just need somewhere to throw your words and not be crucified for it. Caution: avoid manosphere content disguised as "help"—if the pitch includes blaming women, glorifying stoic domination, or selling you a $997 masculinity bootcamp, close the tab and run.

If you're data-driven and need to wrap your logical mind around what's happening before you let yourself feel anything—good. Use that. Here are some of the most reliable, peer-reviewed, and frequently cited sources that grounded this book's research: National Institute of Mental Health (NIMH) for U.S. suicide and depression stats; Centers for Disease Control and Prevention (CDC) for mortality data and the annual National Health Interview Survey; Substance Abuse and Mental Health Services Administration (SAMHSA) for data on substance use and mental illness in men; World Health Organization (WHO) for global trends; American Psychological Association (APA) for white papers on masculinity, therapy, and mental health stigma. Want academic firepower? Dig into journals like The Lancet Psychiatry, Journal of Men's Studies, Psychological Bulletin, or Health Psychology. They're dense but bulletproof when you want to arm yourself with truth instead of TikTok half-facts.

If you're a father, coach, teacher, or human with any influence over young men and boys—your responsibility is sacred. Raise them with vocabulary for their pain. Expose them to books and films where men feel, break, mend, and survive. Start with resources like The Mask You Live In (a game-changing documentary on American masculinity), Raising Cain (a foundational book on boys' emotional development), and For the Love of Men by Liz Plank (a compelling dive into what healthy masculinity looks like without condescension). Supplement with podcasts like Man Enough, The Art of Manliness (for its surprisingly nuanced episodes), and Therapy for Black Men, which offers both insight and solidarity in underserved communities. If you're looking for broader secular philosophical grounding, revisit the stoics—Marcus Aurelius, Seneca, Epictetus—but filter them through the lens of psychological reality. Pair with modern thinkers like Alain de Botton (School of Life), Sam Harris (despite his flaws, his meditation content can be useful), or Mark Manson for digestible, profanity-laced reality checks. If existentialism clicks better than therapy, explore Viktor Frankl's Man's Search for Meaning, Albert Camus's The Myth of Sisyphus, or Irvin Yalom's The Gift of Therapy. Pain needs perspective as much as it needs processing.

Because sometimes healing doesn't start with strategy—it starts with hearing someone else say the thing you thought made you uniquely broken. So here are real, anonymous testimonials gathered (with consent) during the development of this book. Some are raw. All are true.

"I didn't cry when my brother died. I didn't cry at the funeral. I cried six months later because I couldn't figure out how to reset a router and it broke me. That's how grief sneaks up on us."

"EVERY NIGHT I SCROLL Instagram and see motivational quotes telling me to 'be a man' and 'get up and grind.' I'm barely functioning. The grind is killing me."

"I TOLD MY WIFE I WAS depressed and she said, 'You don't look depressed.' I guess because I didn't say it while sobbing or curled into a ball, it didn't count."

"I USED TO THINK THERAPY was for rich white women and guys who couldn't tough it out. Now I know it's for anyone who doesn't want to become a hollow shell of themselves."

"MY DAD DRANK, HIT, and vanished. Now I have a son and no blueprint. I go to therapy so I don't pass that silence on."

"I DIDN'T WANT TO DIE. I just didn't want to keep living like that."

THESE ARE NOT CHERRY-picked. They're ordinary men in extraordinary pain who finally decided their lives mattered more than their image. They are proof that breaking silence doesn't end you—it begins you. And if you're reading this, you now carry their courage forward.

So what now? Use this appendix as a launchpad, not a graveyard of good intentions. Pick one thing. One number to call. One group to try. One book to read. One question to ask a friend. One sentence to say out loud. "I think I need help." "I've been struggling." "I'm tired of faking it." That's the key that unlocks the first door. And once you crack the door open, you'll find that while the hallway might be long and messy, you don't have to walk it alone. Not anymore. Because now you know. Now you've seen it. Now you can't unsee it. The crisis is real. But so is the hope. Not in some far-off utopia where men suddenly evolve into perfectly regulated emotional sages—but here, in the raw middle of the mess, where good men, wounded men, confused men, and silent men finally find the words, the will, and the tools to stay alive.

Print this appendix. Share it. Annotate it. Tape a crisis number to your mirror. Bookmark a therapy directory. Leave a dog-eared book on your friend's doorstep. Invite three guys to a backyard firepit and call it group. No incense. No hand drums. Just truth, laughter, silence, and room for breakdowns. Let it be messy. Let it be sacred in its profanity. Healing rarely looks like a movie montage. Sometimes it looks like crying in your car or texting a stranger or not canceling that appointment. But it's healing. It's real. And it's worth the discomfort.

You deserve to survive this. You don't have to believe in God to believe in your right to feel. You don't need a cross, a creed, or a counselor with a fish symbol on their business card to deserve rest, connection, or redemption. You're allowed to rage and still be redeemable. You're allowed to collapse and still be worth holding. You're allowed to begin again, not because of divine grace, but because you are still here. Still breathing. Still capable of joy. Still worth the effort.

So take what you need. Pass along what you don't. And remember: help is real. Healing is slow. Progress isn't linear. But silence is fatal. This book gave you the words. Now go use them. Say them. Share them. Build something louder.

And if all else fails, just start here:

"Hey. I read something that reminded me of you. Just wanted you to know I'm around if you ever want to talk."

YOU MIGHT JUST SAVE a life. Maybe even your own.

www.ingramcontent.com/pod-product-compliance
Lightning Source LLC
LaVergne TN
LVHW022010200926
848481LV00007B/2319
9798230548553